# ANNUALS

Author
**Patricia Freeman**

Photographer
**John M. Rickard**

Series Concept
**Robert J. Dolezal**

CREATIVE
PUBLISHING
international

Minnetonka, Minnesota

# C O N T E N T S

## GARDENS OF ANNUAL DELIGHT

### Page 1

Tour beautiful garden plantings —
The Beautiful English Border pg. 2
• A Mixed Garden pg. 4 •
Annuals In A Vegetable Garden
pg. 6 • Gifts From Your Garden
pg. 7 • Hot-Climate Annuals pg. 8
• Indoor Annuals pg. 10 • Single-
Flower Plantings pg. 11 •
Annuals In The Shade pg. 12 •
Annuals In Small Spaces pg. 13 •
Spring Annuals pg. 14 • Summer
Annuals pg. 15 • Birds And
Butterflies pg. 17

## A GARDEN CHECKLIST

### Page 18

Decide the scope of your
project—The Anatomy Of
Annuals pg. 20 • Choosing
A Site pg. 22 • Annuals For
Every Purpose pg. 24 •
Scaling The Project pg. 25 •
Containers Versus Beds pg.
26 • Annual Shapes,
Heights, And Textures pg.
27 • Selecting Healthy Plants
pg. 28 • Soil And Fertilizing
pg. 30 • Tools And Materials
pg. 32 • Sources For Plants
And Supplies pg. 34

## ANNUAL PLANNING FLOWCHART

### Page 36

Define your project's needs
by answering some quick
questions designed to save
time and help you create a
shopping list.

## DESIGNING WITH COLOR

### Page 38

Match plantings to your home
and landscape—Using The
Color Palette pg. 40 • Planning
A Seasonal Progression Of
Blooms pg. 43 • Planting For
Foliage pg. 44 • Mixing Scale,
Form, And Texture pg. 46 •
Planning Area Plantings pg. 48
• Planning A Bedding Planting
pg. 49 • Considering
Architectural and Landscape
Features pg. 51 • Planning
Plantings For Pathways pg. 53

## HOW TO PLANT AND GROW ANNUALS

### Page 54

Learn the essentials and get off to a good start—Before Planting pg. 56 • Building A Potting Table pg. 57 • Planting Seeds pg. 60 • Planting In Containers pg. 62 • Direct Sowing Seed Into Beds pg. 64 • Hardening Transplants pg. 66 • Installing An Automatic Drip Watering System pg. 68 • Mulching pg. 70 • Transplanting Into Containers pg. 71

## CARING FOR ANNUALS

### Page 72

A minimum of care with a maximum of results—Supporting Annual Flowers pg. 74 • Watering Needs pg. 75 • Fertilizing Needs pg. 77 • Pinch Pruning pg. 80 • Controlling Pests And Diseases pg. 81

## ENJOYING ANNUALS

### Page 84

Share with friends and family the rewards of growing annuals—Lasting Bouquets pg. 86 • Planning For Color pg. 88 • Planting An Annuals Garden With A Child pg. 89 • The Gift Of Color pg. 90

## ANNUAL PLANTS AND TENDER PERENNIALS

### Page 91

Photographs and complete information for the most commonly used bedding plants, both annuals and those that are tender perennials planted as annuals in many regions. Plants are listed by their most common name, followed by their scientific name, and cross-referenced in the index.

## APPENDIX

### Page 129

Understand how annuals differ from perennial and biennial flowers and locate your microclimate — USDA Plant Hardiness Zones of North America pg. 130 • Climate pg. 131 • Sun Exposure pg. 131 • Approximate Frost-Free Dates pg. 131 • Growth Habits pg. 132 • Soil pg. 132 • Watering pg. 133 • Index pg. 134

# INTRODUCTION

W hether you decide to grow a quarter-acre cutting garden or a single petunia in a pot, you'll discover the pleasure that annual gardening can bring. Some rewards are obvious: beautiful flowers, an improved landscape, and compliments from friends and family. Others are more ineffable: the wonder of seeing nature work its miracles and the satisfaction of watching a living thing respond to your

ministrations. Perhaps best of all are the benefits that stay with you even when you're nowhere near the garden. As you continue gardening you'll notice yourself developing the capacity to observe, to wait, and to enjoy. A pastime that forces you literally to stop and smell the flowers may seem quaint, but the lessons that gardening teaches never will become outdated.

Even the most patient gardeners enjoy seeing the results of their labor in a single season—and annuals provide it. Seeing them grow can be like watching time-lapse photography; compared to more permanent plants they bloom almost instantaneously. With proper deadheading, they produce flowers for weeks and weeks, and for this they demand little in return. Unlike permanent plants that need to establish extensive root systems, annuals have simple needs. They demand nothing more than consistent watering, regular inspection, and occasional fertilizing, mulching, and staking. Most are fairly tolerant of neglect and as a rule are relatively untroubled by pests and disease. They respond eagerly to care, often going on to bloom enthusiastically even after being rescued from death's door.

What kind of relationship you have with your annuals is completely up to you. Deciding which annuals to plant is like choosing a pet: if you have limited time, energy, or abilities, you might love an undemanding hamster more than a rambunctious dog, but if you have the hours and the inclination you may take more joy in raising a puppy. No matter how much time and energy you devote to your plants, they will teach you to enjoy the process as well as the product of your effort—and that's a reward that lasts a lifetime.

*As for marigolds, poppies, hollyhocks, and valorous sunflowers, we shall never have a garden without them, both for their own sake, and for the sake of old-fashioned folks, who used to love them.*

HENRY WARD BEECHER

**Ever-changing colors mark every annuals garden, creating a showcase for your landscape**

Though they last for only a season, annuals are the show stoppers of the garden. From towering sunflowers to diminutive pansies, they bloom in a breathtaking array of shades. Some grow beanstalk tall, others sit demurely at the edge of a border, still others cascade giddily from a container. Their profiles may be rotund or rangy, their textures lacy, velvety, or waxy. They can be stars in their own right, or play a supporting role to perennials, vegetables, bulbs, shrubs, and trees. Carefully selected, they will perform in frost or near-searing heat, sun or shade—even in infertile soil—from the desert to the fringes of the arctic.

It's no wonder annuals are such crowd pleasers—and what a diverse crowd they can please. For the experienced gardener, annuals offer the challenges of growing fussy species and cultivating seedlings for transplant. For the beginner, annuals present the perfect combination of easy care and quick,

# Gardens of Annual Delight

dramatic results. Because annuals are inexpensive—one might even say, dirt cheap—mistakes are never bank-breaking, and success is easily replicated in seasons to come.

Children love the excitement of watching annuals sprout from seeds, especially when those sprouts grow up to reveal cartoon colors, fantastic shapes, or Paul Bunyan proportions. Some of the humblest and most common of annuals are beloved by all for their bewitching fragrances, their ability to attract birds and butterflies, or simply for their reliability.

In the pages that follow, you'll see dozens of inspirational examples of annuals at work and receive all the information you need to create any type of annual garden you may want, no matter what your experience, no matter where you live.

*The beauty of annuals lies in their ability to integrate every landscape feature, from perennials and shrubs to trees, fixtures, and statuary.*

## THE BEAUTIFUL ENGLISH BORDER

A perennial—or perhaps we should say annual—favorite of gardeners, the so-called English border employs annuals to stunning effect. If your taste is informal yet old-fashioned, or you're simply a romantic, this style is for you.

First developed by landscape designers in Great Britain at the turn of the twentieth century, it was an antidote to the rigidly formal garden style that it eventually replaced. The English border looks just right next to a house that's small, quaint, or, well, English.

It has a natural, even playful, look, achieved by combining and juxtaposing a profusion of plantings with different colors, shapes, textures, and heights. Within this natural look, however, is a subtle structure: low plants in front, medium-sized plants behind them, and tall plants in the back; spiky forms are placed to complement rounded ones; colors are equally subtle, tending more toward the pastel rather than the fluorescent.

In Great Britain, border plantings comprise cool-weather annuals that won't tolerate summer heat found in areas much above zone 8. If you live in an area with long, cool summers—or if you want a springtime English border—choose tall larkspur in the back row, old-fashioned mallow at the mid-border, behind poppies and an edging of sweet William [see Designing a Traditional English Border, pg. 50].

You also can create a garden themed around one or two colors by planting, for example, cream- and raspberry-colored pansies, pink globe candytuft, pink and peach Iceland poppies, pink flowering flax, and pink and white foxglove.

If your heart is in England but your yard is in a warmer region, don't despair. Warm-climate dwellers can have English borders, too. If your garden is in a mild-

*Classic English borders comprise plants of various heights, foliage, and color. Where space and circumstances permit, follow the British approach to garden layout—toss a handful of pebbles within each marked area of the bed to determine the planting locations for individual flowers. It results in a natural, free-form arrangement that is eye-catching.*

winter climate, plant your cool-weather annuals in autumn for a winter bloom.

For summer gardens, create an English border with heat-loving annuals such as spider flower in the back row, globe amaranth in the mid-border, and pansies in the front—or start with a backdrop of Mexican sunflowers, which will create a 5–7-foot-high (1.5–2.1-m) background hedge for the rest of your plantings. Their deep-green leaves and bright-orange flowers will harmonize beautifully with mid-border drifts of gold coreopsis.

These and other durable annuals are available in colors that virtually will transport you to the English countryside.

(Above) In a springtime island border that's ideal for cool-climate gardens, tall poppies mark a center point for snapdragons and alyssum. Whenever a group planting stands alone, use its center for the tallest members of the group and ring the perimeter with shorter annuals.

(Left) For edge plantings and borders, follow the classic English border form: tall plants in the rear, occasionally broken by medium-height flowers; medium and low annuals to the front. When fully grown, the border will appear a solid mass of blooms and color.

## A MIXED GARDEN

Like perfect party guests, annuals are delightful in any crowd. If you invite them to mingle with your shrubs, perennials, and bulbs, they'll add interest and long-lasting color to your garden. In a new garden, they'll obligingly fill in for slow-growing permanent companions. Adaptable, undemanding, and fast growing, they'll enhance an established garden—and replace permanent plantings that have faltered.

Annuals can extend the bloom period of your perennial garden at both ends of the season. Early bloomers provide color when most perennials are still taking their long winter's nap; when perennials have finished their show in early summer, warm-season annuals can take over.

In a new garden, annuals are indispensable. A young perennial border can look bare for the first few years; annuals can fill in the gaps. Annual weavers, such as 'Signet' marigold, will thread themselves between permanent plants, giving the border a finished look. Sunflowers and cosmos will add height at the back of a border while your perennials are small, or you can use them to create temporary hedges while you're waiting for immature shrubs to grow and spread. Fast-growing ground-huggers such as sweet alyssum will fill bare spots while your new ground cover grows and fills in.

You can use annuals the way Hollywood directors use stand-ins: try them out in a spot where you're thinking

*(Above) Many perennial flowers and shrubs spend much of the season out of bloom. Draw attention to the flower bed all year long by planting annuals that peak when perennials are still in bud or have long since faded away.*

*(Right) Even evergreen shrubs benefit from annual companions. Often, shrubs are leggy or have bare spots in their lower branches. Annuals are tailor-made for masking these detracting features. Remember to add annual foliage as well as flowers. Coleus, variegated hostas, and other striking plants increase the visual interest in any mixed planting.*

of putting some permanent plants and see how you like the effect. With much less money and soil preparation, you'll be able to tell whether the arrangement of colors, sizes, and shapes you had in mind turns out as you hoped. You also can use annuals as understudies: if a hot spell sends your perennials into summer dormancy, or your garden suffers the ravages of a pet, a storm, or a child with scissors, just bring in some potted annuals and let them take over.

Annuals have a role to play even in a well-established permanent garden. You can pair permanent plants with annuals to create new combinations of color, scale, form, and texture. Verbena and love-in-a-mist will carpet the base of perennials and shrubs; blooming vines such as morning glory can climb the stems of tall perennials; the spikes of larkspur will complement the rounded forms of roses. Given the right conditions, some annuals even will act like perennials by self seeding and reproducing entirely on their own. In fact, gardeners in areas with frost-free winters can treat self-sowing annuals like perennials. Elsewhere, a combination of climate, light, and soil will determine how reliably self sowers reproduce. If you choose native and naturalized species that are well adapted to your area, they'll probably come back to complement your permanent plantings year after year.

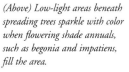

*(Above) Low-light areas beneath spreading trees sparkle with color when flowering shade annuals, such as begonia and impatiens, fill the area.*

*(Left) In large landscapes, annual plantings establish edges and create definition between areas used for different purposes. They minimize maintenance where permanent landscape features, such as mowing strips and walled planters, might be disturbed by surface roots.*

## ANNUALS IN A VEGETABLE GARDEN

If there were a horticultural prom, vegetables probably would not be invited—let's face it, broccoli tastes better than it looks. Pair them with annuals, and vegetables join the party. Even the early colonists, who had little time for frippery, adorned their utilitarian gardens with favorite old-world annuals such as marigolds and primroses. Those are still fine choices for bedecking the vegetable patch. Try mixing a few annual standbys such as pansies and marigolds with your carrots and lettuce for a charmingly colorful little plot. Dress up tomatoes, eggplants, and squash with annual dahlias. Bring out the best in a bed of bell peppers with some zinnias or a planting of poppies.

*Nasturtiums are a favorite for edging many gardens—its flowers are edible as a bonus.*

Adding annuals also is the perfect way to vary the skyline of your vegetable garden. Sow a rear guard of sunflowers, or plant a row of marigolds in the foreground and one of cosmos in the back. Plant spider flowers alongside a trellis of hyacinth or scarlet runner bean for even more variety. Cannas and corn make an engagingly statuesque combination.

Vegetables that are beautiful look even better coupled with annuals of contrasting color. The deep-purple leaves of red mustard or purple basil, for example, will shine handsomely among orange marigolds. If elegance is your goal, try marigolds and gloriosa daisies with yellow bell peppers, or cockscomb with red peppers.

*Even sky-high corn can meet its match when it is paired with giant sunflowers. Tall, sturdy annuals also make great supports for climbing vegetable and flower vines: sweet pea, morning glory, or scarlet runner bean.*

Of course, appearances aren't everything; in the vegetable garden annuals are more than just pretty faces. Many people believe that nasturtiums and marigolds planted alongside vegetables will ward off insect pests. Though frequently tested, that theory has never been proven, but an interplanting of flowers definitely will attract beneficial insects such as ladybugs, parasitic wasps, lacewings, and syrphid flies that feed on vegetable pests. Flowering annuals also appeal to pollinating insects, and they draw birds and butterflies to the vegetable garden.

Finally, for good measure, many annual flowers can accompany their vegetable neighbors right into the salad bowl and be eaten along with them.

### EDIBLE ANNUAL FLOWERS

Tuberous begonia
English daisy
Ornamental cabbage and kale
  (flowers, not leaves)
Calendula
Spider flower
Pinks
Hyacinth bean

Sunflower
  (seeds, not flowers)
Scarlet runner bean
  (seeds and young pods also are edible)
Salvia
Marigolds (especially 'Signet' cultivar)
Nasturtium
Pansy

*While the theory that marigolds ward off insect pests has never been proven, they do attract pollinating insects to young vegetable plantings, dress up the patch while they're at it, and even can be harvested as an addition to the salad bowl.*

What gift can you give the person who has everything? A little of the green stuff is always welcome—no, not cash, but something lovelier: annuals in a container. Elegant, inexpensive, and custom-made, a living bouquet is as satisfying to give as it is to receive. A gift of annuals makes an appropriate offering for any occasion, so go ahead: create a container planting for your best friend's housewarming, your boss' birthday party, or the helpful neighbor who took care of your pet while you were away.

Container gardens mature quickly, bloom for many weeks, and require only modest upkeep; include a few fragrant annuals and they will smell delightful, too. If you choose your plants carefully, they will grow anywhere except in very deep shade so advise the recipient to place the garden in a sunny location. Better yet, include care instructions along with the gift. Compact annuals are the best choice to occupy and complete a gift-size container garden. The combinations are practically limitless, as is the potential for designing a planting that suits the individual as well as a particular indoor or outdoor site.

Are you wondering what would complement the new home your supervisor just bought? Consider a single-flower planting of something dignified yet dramatic, like ivy geranium. How about a mixed-foliage arrangement for your friend with the sleek, uncluttered condo? A relative's quaint little cottage would be the perfect home for a container filled with cascading annuals such as petunia, lobelia, and creeping zinnia, together with upright ones such as moss rose, annual dahlia, and flossflower. You even can create arrangements for challenging conditions and recipients: a combination of shade-loving annuals to brighten a college student's lightless studio apartment, or a few low-maintenance selections for the friend blessed with a not-so-green thumb.

If you're unsure exactly what annuals to use or how to arrange and plant them, never fear. The process of creating a gift of beautiful annuals is pretty much the same as that used for creating an outdoor garden, except that the smaller space will make the task even easier.

There's also helpful advice on how to create pleasing combinations of color, shape, and texture [see Chapter Two: *A Garden Checklist*].

[see Chapter Two: *A Garden Checklist*].

## GIFTS FROM YOUR GARDEN

*(Left) Flowering plants make welcome gifts that you can create from your garden. Choose an attractive container or basket, and line it with a waterproof insert; they're sold in a variety of sizes at many garden and retail stores.*

*Remember annual plants include those prized for their foliage in addition to their flowers, such as dusty miller (above) and bells of Ireland (left).*

## HOT-CLIMATE ANNUALS

Most annuals adore sun—on the average, they need at least six hours each day. Some climates, and some gardens, have too much of a good thing. Just ask anyone who has tried to plant snapdragons in a desert-hot summer, or placed petunias in the reflected heat of a cinderblock wall. Fortunately, there are many annuals that cheerfully tolerate temperatures that would wilt less stalwart flowers. A few truly heat-resistant varieties face the hot sun as resolutely as a teenager determined to get a tan.

You aren't just limited to these standbys. Add an exotic note with the chenillelike flowers of love-lies-bleeding. Create a spectacle with the comic-book blooms of crested cockscomb or amaranth. Bring in some fabulous foliage, such as summer cypress, a fireplug-shaped specimen with feathery leaves that turn flame-red at summer's end.

There are heat-loving annuals for every spot in the summer garden. Statuesque candidates for the back of the border include spider flower, which looks refreshed even on hot, humid days, and Mexican sunflower, a South American native and among the most heat-resistant

*(Above) Extended spells of very hot weather can tire or harm your annual plantings. When heat is forecast, water thoroughly in late afternoon, allowing time for foliage to dry before dusk.*

*(Right) Most heat-loving annuals have woody stems and deep, matted root systems that allow them to glean water and resist wilting. Such colonies expand at their margins; remember to thin and replant the centers as their blooms become less productive.*

of all annuals. If your background is a wall or chain-link fence, tropical vines such as morning glory can transform it into a curtain of color.

For the middle of a tropical border, there are some highly adaptable sun worshippers from which to choose. Globe amaranth stands up to humidity as well as high temperatures, and its cloverlike flowers are excellent for cutting. The wonderful annual vinca tolerates not only heat but also drought, humidity, and air pollution. Coreopsis, a heat-tolerant annual native to the North American prairie, thrives even in low-nutrient soil.

For a heat-loving front line, edge with creeping zinnia, moss rose, and the compact globe amaranth.

Creating a successful hot-weather garden is more than just a matter of choosing the right annuals for the job. Prepare the soil very carefully and space your plants closer together than is typically recommended to help shade the soil. Plant early in the season and select an area that gets morning sun rather than the potent rays of afternoon sun.

Before you buy any plants described as heat resistant, check Annual Plants and Tender Perennials [see pg. 91] and consult with your garden retailer to make sure they're suited to your particular region. Also, take a chance on some of the many sun-loving annuals that aren't specifically bred for heat resistance: many can survive all but the most searing temperatures if planted in excellent soil and kept well watered.

*(Above) For best results with cosmos, plant closely and provide support as they grow to full height. They bear a succession of flowers at the terminal buds ending each foliage limb.*

*The intensity of sunlight is increased near light-colored, heat-retaining walls and fences. In cool climates, use this to your advantage by planting heat-loving species; in hot climates, reserve such locations for your most durable annuals.*

## INDOOR ANNUALS

Wouldn't it be wonderful if you could fill your house with your favorite blooms and have them last more than a week? Sound too good to be true? Well, this is no fantasy. All you have to do is grow a few annuals indoors.

All types of annuals, especially shade lovers, can bring a little spring inside. Brighten a corner with some daisies. Pansies would be cheery in the breakfast nook. Petunias take on a new look when planted in containers and come in a staggering array of colors. Lisianthus gives a room a romantic look. Sweet alyssum will perfume the house for an entire season. No matter what your favorite plant [see Annual Plants and Tender Perennials, pg. 91], you'll develop a new appreciation for it when you're able to enjoy it up-close and personal.

Outdoors, every annual has its season, but the indoor gardener is never at the mercy of the calendar. With correct lighting, many types of flowers will bloom indoors during winter days when many gardeners are forced into hibernation. Geraniums will bear flowers for most of the winter if planted in summer, and they are easy to grow from seedlings. Blanket flower can warm up the chilly season with its primary colors, and it tolerates underwatering. If you don't mind a little more maintenance, try the sublime China aster, which, with supplemental light, can be grown for winter bloom and comes in several dwarf forms that are perfect for containers. The many varieties of coleus, grown for its kaleidoscopic foliage, never lose their color.

You quickly and easily can fill your home with flowers by potting garden-ready plants from your local nursery or home garden center. It's possible to start your indoor garden from seed; however, you'll need grow lights—special fluorescent light bulbs that emit the type of light conducive to plant growth—to start some of the more demanding annuals. Others may require nothing more than a sunny windowsill [see Planting a Windowbox, pg. 52]. Whatever your circumstances—whether your gardening is limited to indoors, you live in an area where the growing season is shorter than a television miniseries, or you just want to enjoy your Johnny-jump-ups at other than snail's-eye level in the garden—there's always a good reason to grow annuals indoors.

*(Above) Cut flowers from your garden are a bonus whenever flowers are prolific. For a more sustained decor, plant annuals in showy containers for display in your home. A few hours of selection and planting will provide months of enjoyment.*

*Indoor plants need four essentials: lots of sunlight, regular watering, frequent feeding, and good drainage. Choose sunny locations to minimize legginess and increase blooms. Water whenever the soil dries, and always allow it to become dry before watering. Fertilize weekly. Choose containers with ample drains and avoid allowing the plant to stand in water.*

# SINGLE-FLOWER PLANTINGS

With so many fabulous annuals from which to choose, it's tempting to cram the garden with everything from alyssum to zinnia. For sheer impact, a more effective strategy may be to plant just one kind of flower. Nature herself knows that nothing is more breathtaking than an expanse of azure-blue forget-me-nots, and who can forget the field of poppies that put Dorothy and her friends to sleep on the way to the Emerald City? The Victorians were mad for putting single-plant masses of annuals in their orderly beds; they often planted a single type of flower by the hundreds. Whether you have a vista to cultivate or you wish to punctuate the far side of the lawn with a splash of color, you can make a bold statement with a single-flower planting. As a bonus, designing your garden will be a snap.

Those lucky enough to have a large, open area to fill should choose meadow annuals as an attractive and practical option for a single-flower planting. Plants such as cornflower and California poppy are easy-care choices, and, in areas that do not freeze, they reseed themselves and bloom again every year. Go traditional and plant cornflower in classic blue, or you can choose from pink, white, purple, or red. If you select poppies, a red carpet will give you that south-of-France look, but you also can select brilliant shades of yellow, scarlet, pink, orange, or white.

Where summers are very warm and the soil tends to be lean and dry, blanket flower, coreopsis, and black-eyed Susan are excellent choices. Coreopsis blooms all summer and produces a lovely, undulating sea of yellow, orange, maroon, or red when planted in masses. Sunset-colored blanket flower, which grows as a wildflower in much of the southern United States, also is effective when massed. The 'Orange Bedder' variety of black-eyed Susan is especially recommended for planting a mass bedding.

Though annuals perform magnificently in a garden ensemble, they can be first-rate soloists as well. When you want to cause a sensation, give star billing to your favorite annual, then sit back and watch the show.

*(Top) A striking seasonal ground cover will result when low-growing, mat-forming annuals are planted in a group. Choose well-defined beds for maximum effect.*

*(Below) Massed flower plantings look their best when seeds are sown directly into the soil at the site. This ensures that all of the plants will grow and mature at the same time.*

## ANNUALS IN THE SHADE

*(Top) Hanging baskets make ideal shade residents—just remember to take them out into the full sun a day or two a week to ensure good foliage development and strong stems.*

*(Below) Permanent shade plantings require careful selection of annuals able to make do with less sunlight.*

If you've always thought the only way to bring color to the shady areas of your yard was to put the lawn furniture there, take heart. Just choose the right annuals and you can create any kind of garden you want.

Sure, the selection of annuals for a shady garden is more limited than for a sunny one, but rest assured that there is a shade-tolerant annual for nearly every purpose. Early-flowering, cool-season varieties can cover a shadowed space with color even when the weather is frosty. Popular favorites such as pansy and Johnny-jump-up perform well, as does old-fashioned honesty. For a delicate effect, combine baby blue eyes or pale-blue forget-me-nots with yellow-and-white meadow foam. When the weather warms up, you can set a tropical mood with exotic foliage plants such as coleus, caladium, polka dot plant, plectranthus, and 'New Guinea' impatiens. Combine them with glossy wax begonias for a lush effect.

Regardless of which colors appeal to you, you'll find shade-tolerant annuals in plenty of pleasing hues. If you happen to be partial to pale tones, shaded spaces are definitely the place for them. Bush violet is one of several annuals that can serve as a cool accent in a shady corner: others are lobelia; viscaria, with blue or violet flowers atop willowy stems; or blue woodruff, a fragrant annual whose blossoms open bright blue and gradually fade to pale lavender.

Even some plants known for their sun-loving ways can be coaxed to bloom in partial shade, especially if given humus-rich soil and plenty of moisture. Statuesque spider flower, for example, will produce fewer flowers if it gets less than a full day of sun, but each bloom will last longer. Plant it as a backdrop for nicotiana, larkspur, butterfly flower, and wallflower, and you have a shady English border. As you can see in Annual Plants and Tender Perennials [see pg. 91], you have quite an array of choices if your planting site gets fewer than four hours of full sun in the morning and two more in the afternoon.

Planting a garden in full shade is trickier, but you can still get good results by selecting annuals that are die-hard shade lovers such as impatiens, America's most popular bedding plant, and begonias, the reigning champion of shade tolerance.

## ANNUALS IN SMALL SPACES

There are any number of reasons to think small when you garden. Perhaps you live in an apartment and your planting site is a windowbox, or you live in the suburbs and you want to turn your patio into a tropical oasis. Perhaps infirmity prevents you from tilling the back forty, or you're a beginning gardener looking for a manageable project. Maybe you just haven't much time. Whatever prompts you to downsize your garden, use annuals to create a bit of paradise in a small plot or a container.

Growing annuals in containers is the perfect way to begin gardening and a satisfying way to apply your experience if you're a veteran of the weed wars. To start with, making the bed is a more manageable task, as is designing it, since you'll get best results using only two to four different types of plants. In addition, because space is limited, so are gardening chores—and opportunities to avoid common pitfalls.

Your chance of success is improved by every aspect of container planting being controllable: you can ensure perfect soil quality and moisture levels, even regulate temperature, sun, and shade by moving pots from one place to another. The portability of many container gardens also makes them versatile decorating tools and allows you to move them out of sight when their blooms are spent or bring them indoors before the first frost strikes. You even can find plenty of container annuals that happily will spend their entire lives inside.

Container plantings can be designed as simply or as elaborately as your time and creativity dictates. Single-flower plantings are perfect for pots. Moss rose, periwinkle, impatiens, begonias, and violas, for example, can all hold their own as soloists.

Those who feel more ambitious can design a complex container planting using trailing, climbing, and upright annuals. For a shade-loving hanging basket, combine bush violet, viscaria, and begonias, then add a solitary polka dot plant for a focal point and a black-eyed Susan vine trailing down.

Whether your home is a studio apartment or a country estate, you probably have a place for a little gem of a garden or a picture-perfect container planting. If you haven't already, make space for one this season and you'll see how beautiful small can be.

*(Top) Window and railing flower boxes complete a home's appearance. If access for maintenance is a problem, install a drip irrigation line to each planter.*

*(Bottom) Locations abound for those with limited space for in-ground gardens. Stark walls in sunny locations are ideal sites for fixed and hanging planters—small-space gardening at its vertical best.*

## SPRING ANNUALS

Many beloved spring blossoms are cool-season annuals. Pansies, poppies, English daisies, Johnny-jump-ups, forget-me-nots—these are the flowers that herald the arrival of spring and persevere even through unexpected frost.

Spring annuals are incredibly versatile. They can complement bulbs, fill in for perennials that aren't yet in bloom, or make a colorful spectacle in an all-annual bed or border.

Start spring with an early blooming of old favorites or try them in combinations. Combining spring annuals with bulbs is a popular option for good reason: few sights are as pretty as a bed of purple pansies with yellow daffodils. Pair two complementary or contrasting kinds of annuals for a striking effect.

Spring annuals are as adaptable as they are beautiful. You can grow them all summer in areas where the weather doesn't get too hot. You can sow them in autumn for a winter bloom in frost-free climates and for spring bloom in areas where temperatures don't fall too far below freezing. In chillier locales, you can extend the life of your garden by planting spring favorites at summer's end for late fall color.

Even in the coldest gardens, a few extremely hardy varieties may be planted in autumn and will survive the winter as seeds: try sowing larkspur, corn poppy, and chrysanthemum in late autumn for a beautiful blue, red, and gold combination the following spring.

*(Above) Springtime profusions of flowers mark the true start of the gardening season. If the weather remains constant, flowers planted early frequently bloom on as late as mid-summer.*

*Choose a palette that complements the season: warm pinks, reds, oranges, and yellows herald spring.*

# SUMMER ANNUALS

When the summer sun begins to shine, the most famous and the most flamboyant performers in the annual garden take center stage. Such enduring stars as zinnias, marigolds, petunias, geraniums, and impatiens appear in early summer and put on a show that lasts until the first fall frost. Multicolored annual dahlias, maroon castor bean plants, fiery-red celosias, limeade-green coleuses, and many other amazing annuals are warm-season attractions as well. For sheer spectacle and truly astonishing variety, the summer annual garden is unsurpassed.

Summer annuals come in a rainbow of colors. Do you love flaming orange? Plant some Mexican sunflower. Are you fond of fuchsia? Try cosmos 'Sensation.' Would you like a neon-sign effect? Try the dahlia 'Flashlight' series. On the other hand, if you're partial to blues and purples, there are lobelias, browallias, salvias, and felicias to soothe you. Mix the softer blues with pinks and yellows for a pastel planting, or create a classic blue-and-yellow border by combining yellow cosmos, dahlias, and French marigolds with indigo-blue salvia, flossflower, and dwarf morning glory. For a crisp, clean look, go completely white. Many summer favorites, such as spider flower, cosmos, and petunias

*Summer flowers are planted once soil temperatures have warmed sufficiently to make their growth certain. Such annuals require somewhat longer growth cycles and prefer lots of warm, sunny days. They reward you with lots of big, showy blooms.*

*(Above) Petunias span the summer season with continuous, prolific production of flowers. Because they expend so much energy, be sure to fertilize them at least monthly for each month of growth.*

*(Bottom left) Many species of annuals sport double or even triple flowers, making them as showy as many perennials.*

*(Bottom right) Count on compact growth from clustering annual plants to build mounds of flowers around garden fixtures, lights, paths, and perennial shrubs.*

have white cultivars [see Using a Color Wheel, pg. 41].

Summer annuals also come in an array of shapes and sizes, so you can put them to work all over your yard. Create some privacy by planting a tall screen of sunflowers. Dress up an unadorned plot with a ground cover of lobelia. Camouflage an unsightly fence with morning glory.

Bring armloads of dahlias, zinnias, geraniums, and snapdragons indoors as cut flowers [see Lasting Bouquets, pg. 86]. Perfume the yard with petite sweet alyssum or scented petunias. For night fragrance and blooms, plant nicotiana or a hedge of four o'clock.

There are so many kinds of summer annuals that even beginning gardeners can have a colorful crop of flowers that will bloom all summer: many annuals, including begonias, petunias, periwinkles, scarlet salvias, and heliotrope, practically care for themselves, and even the most common summer annuals are appreciated for their good looks, prolific blooms, and winning ways. Whether you're a weekend weeder or willing to nursemaid a fussy salpiglossis plant for a season, annuals have a place in your summer garden.

## BIRDS AND BUTTERFLIES

Birds and butterflies are drawn to some flowers the way—well, the way bees are drawn to nectar. You can plant an all-annual bird-and-butterfly garden, or use selected annuals in combination with shrubs and perennials to attract beautiful airborne creatures. To invite birds and butterflies into your yard, first provide a source of water. A container 2 feet (60 cm) wide will bring flying wildlife to any garden, even an urban balcony. In the garden, a birdbath will do nicely, but if you want birds to use it, also provide some sort of platform that can serve as an avian landing strip.

Next, plant splashes of intensely colored tubular flowers as a buffet for hummingbirds. Hummers prefer red flowers but also like vivid shades of purple, orange, and yellow. Butterflies are drawn to all types of annuals, so just about any garden you plant is likely to have some flowers that will meet with butterfly approval.

Scent is a powerful attractant for both hummingbirds and butterflies. Sweet-smelling four-o'-clock, which blooms in the late afternoon, will attract butterflies and hummingbirds by day and moths after night has fallen, and fragrant, evening-scented stock will receive frequent visits from winged passersby despite its decidedly unprepossessing blossoms.

Songbirds will visit your garden if you give them a high observation perch so they can study the territory and the water supply from a comfortable distance. You may have permanent plantings that will serve this purpose, but annual vines also make a safe place for birds to land. Once songbirds have found a vantage point, they will descend into the garden looking for seeds to eat. They particularly love tall annuals such as cosmos and sunflower. You also will host a variety of diners with such mid-size offerings as marigold, black-eyed Susan, and coreopsis and low growers such as forget-me-not and moss rose.

After your flowers have bloomed, skip some of your deadheading chores so plants will set seed and provide plenty of bird food. With the hours you save, you'll have time to smell the flowers, too.

*(Top) Dried seeds, whether of sunflowers or other annuals, are a draw for many species of wild birds. They provide a natural source of food even after the gardening season has ended.*

*(Bottom left) Butterflies are attracted to bright-colored flowers, especially those with reservoirs of nectar or lots of nutritious pollen.*

*(Bottom right) Avian acrobats that delight children of all ages fill gardens planted with bright annuals. Hummingbirds are powerful flyers despite their minute size—many species travel thousands of miles when migrating in spring and during early autumn.*

I nspired by the ideas in the last chapter and the information in the encyclopedia, you're ready to head down to your local nursery and come back with a car full of annual seedlings or a shopping bag full of seeds. Wait. Don't slip into your gardening clogs just yet.

Many a gardener has observed firsthand the less-than-stellar performance of annuals planted in the wrong place at the wrong time. That's why this chapter is devoted to a checklist that begins by asking you to think about your climate and gardening timetable. After taking a good look at the prevailing conditions in your garden—including sun and shade, drainage and hardscape—you'll be able to plant annuals that will thrive. Since your choice of annuals depends on how you intend to use them, the checklist will start you thinking about the purpose of your garden: do you want to grow a few flowers in pots, or are you landscaping an entire yard?

**Plan, prepare, and choose form and function— they're the keys to every successful garden**

# A Garden Checklist

Next, we'll pose some questions that will help you decide how big a gardening project you can manage. Then you'll consider the form, flowers, and texture of the annuals you'd like to plant to determine whether they're compatible with your chosen site. The final checklist questions will tell you how to examine your soil before you plant and give you a working knowledge of all the things you'll need to create your annual garden, including how to choose healthy nursery plants, what you'll want in your gardening toolkit, and where to purchase seeds, plants, and tools.

*Before leaving your garden gate, make some decisions about the flowers that you wish to plant. Your choices now will set into motion the steps you'll take, the plants you'll buy, the tools and materials you'll choose, the time and effort you'll expend, and the garden you'll grow.*

## THE ANATOMY OF ANNUALS

When you were a child, you probably called annuals "flowers." This designation, albeit unscientific, neatly describes their biological destiny. While permanent plants such as shrubs and perennials flower for only a few weeks, annuals bloom with lightning speed and keep going for up to five months. They have to flower at such a frenetic pace because they don't have much time to reproduce themselves. As their name implies, they complete their entire life cycle in a single year or less: they germinate, bloom in a blaze of glory, set seed, and die at a point when their longer-lived perennial neighbors remain puny and plain. That's why you'll plant a new crop of annuals each season, except in cases where they self sow.

Practically speaking, any plant that you intend to keep in your garden for a year or less is an annual. However, not all the candidates you'll consider are true annuals that go from tiny sprout to the compost pile in under twelve months. Some are perennials that behave like annuals in many climates. Others are biennials with life cycles of two years, growing foliage in the first season, then blooming and dying in the second. If you want to use biennials as annuals, start them indoors, purchase them as second-season transplants, or find quick-blooming cultivars and sow them early. A few perennials mentioned have tuberous roots or rhizomes that die in cold weather. You can replant them each year or dig up their roots and bring them inside for replanting the following season [see Appendix, pg. 129].

Annuals are divided further into three major categories, according to how well they tolerate freezing temperatures: hardy (able to survive repeated hard frosts), half-hardy (able to survive light frost), and tender (killed by frost). Hardy specimens are so frost tolerant that they even may be planted in autumn to winter over and provide

### ANNUAL FLOWER ANATOMY

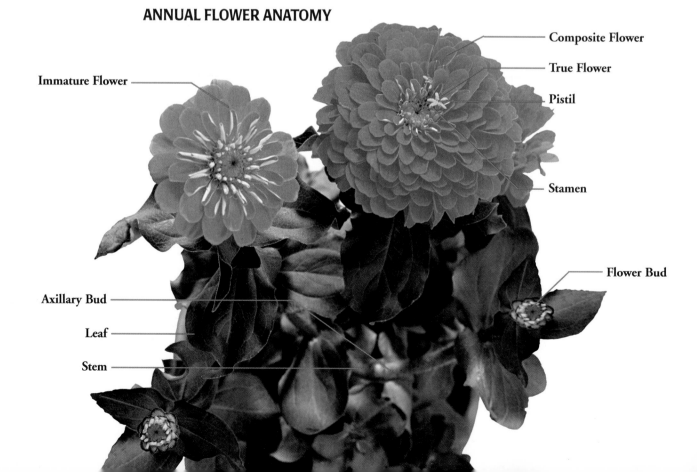

Immature Flower

Composite Flower

True Flower

Pistil

Stamen

Flower Bud

Axillary Bud

Leaf

Stem

flowers the following spring. As you might expect, most warm-season annuals are frost tender while most cool-season plants suffer in excessive heat. Warm-season annuals prefer the warm soil and air temperatures that characterize summer in most of North America. Cool-season annuals, on the other hand, fade and even die in the intense heat of mid-summer in many climates and must be planted very early in spring. A few cool-season selections are so fussy that they're intolerant of both frost and heat—they do well only in areas with a long, mild growing season.

Why is knowing such botanical detail important? Simply, it can prevent you from experiencing the number one cause of annual-garden failure: planting the right annual at the wrong time. To avoid ending up with annual heartbreak, the first thing you need to ask yourself is: Where am I? This is a practical question, not an existential one. If you plan to grow pansies, it makes a difference whether you're in Portland, Maine; Winnipeg, Canada; or Puerto Vallarta, Mexico. The good news is, regardless of where you live, you can grow most any kind of annual, providing you plan around your growing season and climate [see U.S.D.A. Plant Hardiness Zones, pg. 130].

After you've determined the length of your growing season, you'll need to know something about the prevailing temperatures in your region. Just because Portland, Oregon, and Charleston, South Carolina, both have long growing seasons doesn't mean both cities will have the same annual gardens at the same time. The trick is to match the type of annual you're planting with the time of year it will thrive in your area. In some cases, growing the annuals you want may require you to start them indoors. You still will be able to keep all these annuals on your list—providing you know your climate and are realistic about how much time you have to give them.

*There are several types of flowers besides annuals. (Left) Foxglove is an example of a biennial flower. It sprouts and grows foliage in its first year, blooms and sets seed in its second, and then dies. Plant biennials as second-year nursery starts if you want their color added to your annual garden. (Center) Perennial flowers, such as Serbian bellflower, grow and set flowers each year, then go dormant through winter. Occasionally they are killed by severe weather. (Right) Bulb plants like daffodils—including corms, tubers, and rhizomes—bloom each year from root divisions set out in autumn in mild-winter climates, or in early spring in areas with severe winters.*

## CHOOSING A SITE

Even though your childhood home in Connecticut and your city apartment have the same climate and growing season, you're probably not going to plant the same annual garden in both places. The sunflowers that look so majestic at the back of an expansive lot aren't the best choice for that windowbox on an urban balcony. For that matter, they also won't do well in the shady border on the north side of the Connecticut yard, either. That's why the second step in planning your annual garden is to ask yourself questions about the planting site.

Whether you plant your annuals in a macramé basket or a meadow, the location you choose simultaneously will limit and expand your gardening possibilities. Should you live, for example, in a city apartment where your annual garden consists of a terra-cotta planter on a sunny kitchen table, your planting site will not accommodate a 10-foot-tall (3-m) castor bean plant.

Instead, get close to some tiny treasures, such as nolana and nemesia, that would hardly gain notice in larger surroundings. Scented flowers also will smell sweeter in a smaller space, with no wind or heat to dissipate their fragrance.

In addition, a smaller space can lend a fresh appreciation for the beauty of such "common" annuals as petunias and sweet alyssum, or allow you to nurture some selections, such as lisianthus, that would be high maintenance in anything other than a confined, controlled environment [see Transplanting into Containers, pg. 71].

If your garden is on a balcony, terrace, or rooftop, consider sun, shade, and heat carefully

*(Top) Sites for annual plantings can be as simple as a row of pots, or as expansive as an entire field of flowers.*

*(Left) Plant annuals in locations where they are least expected for greater impact. By dedicating new areas to annual flower beds, your landscape will increase in both interest and diversity.*

when choosing annuals to plant. Put begonias in the pitiless sun that can strike a roof garden, and they will toast. Put gazania in the shade of the balcony above yours, and it will bear scraggly blooms that refuse to open. Instead, put the begonias under the balcony and the gazania in the direct sun.

You also may be able to alter your planting site a bit. For example, a trellis covered with potted annual vines serves to shade your other container plantings, or a shade cover will improve conditions on your easy-bake rooftop.

For a country or suburban landscape, planting considerations are no less measured. Will your annuals be sharing space with trees or shrubs? While light for your annuals may be adequate in springtime, by summer the overstory of foliage from trees and shrubs can make the area too shady for the flowers you've chosen, and the roots of larger plants may compete with your annuals for water or nutrients.

Will you be putting annuals near a wall, patio, deck, or pool? Make sure that the annuals you've chosen can tolerate the reflected heat of your hardscape.

Is your garden subject to high humidity or constant rains? You may avoid zinnias and other mildew-prone plants and choose, instead, monkey flowers, forget-me-nots, meadow foam, and other annuals that enjoy moist environments. Even if you have no time to prepare your soil, moss rose and sweet

*Tender perennials, such as the climbing vine clematis, often are grown as single-season annuals in many regions with cold-winter climates. Though they live comfortably for decades in warm areas, they will require annual replanting where winters include hard freezes.*

alyssum will tolerate such hardship, happily growing between the cracks of a stone walkway, and looking beautiful while they're about it.

In the spirit of Thoreau, who advised his readers never to take a job that would require them to buy new clothes, choose annuals that are right for the occasion. Examine your planting site, pick annuals that will fit your conditions, and they will be the life of the party.

*(Left) Although gardeners tend to bed their annuals in bunches, sunny locations along walkways and paths also make excellent sites for small communities of plants that add color to the passage.*

*(Right) Foundation plantings soften the otherwise hard and uncompromising nature of stone and concrete.*

## ANNUALS FOR EVERY PURPOSE

Imagine that you're having a celebration at your house next month and you need to turn your yard into a garden showpiece in time for the event. Now, consider instead that your goal is to block the view of the garbage cans. Thinking about the function your plants will serve makes it easier to pick the right ones.

If you're just trying to hide an eyesore, your decision will be a simple matter of choosing plants that are the appropriate size and shape: a trellis covered with morning glory, for example, or a dense, 3-foot-tall (90-cm) row of burning bush. If you're landscaping a small space, you can avoid a cluttered, jarring effect by choosing just a few kinds of annuals. In the reverse case of an empty yard, you may have multiple objectives: a hedge of castor bean will create privacy; self-seeding annuals, such as poppies for spring and sunflowers for summer, save time.

When you've decided which annuals suit your purpose, consider how soon you need them. When time is not an issue, expand your plant palette and minimize your expense by planting seeds. Annuals do grow fast but perhaps not as fast as you'd prefer. If you simply must have instant color by next Tuesday—perhaps a favorite relative is arriving for a visit—you can achieve that effect, as long as you're willing to spring for nursery transplants.

Some of your annual choices may not be destined for the garden. Your purpose may be to grow them for gifts—if so, the choice of plants will be determined by their adaptability to container living [see Transplanting into Containers, pg. 71]. You instead may want your annuals to double as winter houseplants, in which case look for varieties well adapted to life indoors [see Indoor Annuals, pg. 10]. Whatever function you have in mind for your annuals, you'll find plenty to suit your purposes. Pick the right annual for the job, and you're on your way to success.

*(Top) Living plants in decorative containers bring the garden indoors for parties, gatherings, or other social occasions. Remember to make most of these temporary visitors, however; unless abundant light is available to continue their growth, they will soon lose vigor and cease blooming.*

*(Left) Many times, unused areas of the yard collect debris and become unsightly; use annuals to create the illusion of a pathway where no destination exists. Curved plantings lend mystery and entice the eye.*

*(Right) Tall plants with subtle flowers and filigreed foliage mask and hide by breaking up the outline of such utilitarian fixtures as gas meters, utility poles, or air conditioner units.*

# SCALING THE PROJECT

Gardening, like any relationship, is a commitment. Its extent depends on whether you are seeking lifelong passion or coffee and conversation on alternate Thursdays. Similarly, before you plant your annual garden, you should consider how much time, space, and resources you have available to devote to it.

Start by asking yourself how many hours you realistically can spend creating and caring for your garden. Are you able to weed for an entire day if it pleases you, or do you work an 80-hour week as a partner in a multinational law firm? Are you home during the growing season, or do you spend weeks away during summer?

Next, consider your experience as a gardener. Even if you have plenty of time on your hands, you may want to keep your project small at first, to ensure its success. Health and mobility are factors, too: you might not mind bouncing a shovel off a bed of hardpan for an afternoon, or you may prefer to pay someone else to do the job.

Think about your budget as well. Can you afford the in-ground watering system that would be advisable for the magnificent mass planting you're imagining? Are there sufficient funds for all the nursery plants you'll need to buy for the instant annual border you have in mind, or are seeds a better answer?

Your own attributes and inclinations are only part of the equation. The other factor is your space. If you have to turn sideways to squeeze between the house and the fence, your annuals choices still will be abundant. If, by contrast, you have an acre of land, you'll have the option of planting a large number and variety of annuals.

Consider also whether your yard is well prepared for planting annuals. Can you use existing flower beds, or must you dig up turf to create space? Is your soil already rich with humus and fertilizer, or do you need to plan for those additions? Do you have a watering system in place, or will you have to create one?

Once you've taken stock of your desires, space, and soil, your final step is to consider how much time your garden will demand—large gardens do not necessarily require more time. If you can devote only a couple of hours a week, choose annuals that don't mind if you occasionally forget to feed or water them.

In a perfect world, your vision of your garden would match exactly your time and ability to create it. In the real world, the annual garden of your dreams probably will be more like a good marriage, intimately gratifying but requiring occasional compromise.

*Planting and maintaining your garden can be a part-time job, a weekend pastime, or an occasional fritter—it all depends on your choice of plants and the size of your plantings.*

## CONTAINERS VERSUS BEDS

You probably already know where you'd like to plant annuals: that bald spot under the big tree could use some help, and it would be nice to have a little color by the deck. Before you start digging, consider whether you'd rather grow your plants directly in the garden soil or in containers.

A bed certainly is the best place for big annuals. It's also the site to grow annuals in quantity for a cutting garden, mass planting, or carpet bed. If it's flexibility you want, containers gain the edge. Many containers allow you to move plants from one place to another, bringing them to center stage for a week or two, then setting them out of sight as flowers fade. Containers also call attention to flowers that otherwise might go unnoticed or raise the blooms of fragrant flowers to nose level.

*(Right) Raised-bed planters are the ultimate when defining a planting bed. They also allow gardening to proceed where soil is poor or drainage is a problem.*

*(Bottom) Vacation absences threaten container plants by interrupting regular supplies of water. Install slow-release watering aids during such periods to bridge the gap between ordinary irrigations.*

You also can use containers to grow annuals that would find an in-ground site inhospitable. For instance, if you have a deeply shaded spot, you can move in potted foliage annuals for a few weeks at a time, then treat them to a brighter spot. If your yard has more sand than the Sahara or drainage worse than the Okefenokee, containers give you the option of growing flowers without amending the soil or altering the landscape. Similarly, if the roots of your silver maple have absorbed all nearby soil nutrients, pots of impatiens will brighten the unplantable area.

Planting annuals in containers adds a few extra steps to the process of planning and preparing but saves on stooping and maintenance. You'll need to figure out the depth, shape, and volume of each container to accommodate your plants and consider the material, liners, watering aids, and other auxiliary materials that may be needed. Still, watering and fertilizing a container planting is not as complex as maintaining a flower bed, though those chores must be done more frequently.

Deciding to grow some annuals in containers and others in beds will yield both banquets of blooms and a moveable feast of flowers.

L et's face it—not everyone looks great or feels good in the latest fashions; by the same token, not every yard is enhanced by pansies and petunias. When planning your garden, think about how the forms, flowers, and textures of your desired annuals will fit in with their surroundings, including their companion plants.

Start by imagining how your chosen annuals will look alongside your house. Do you have a stately Georgian manor with a manicured lawn? Even though you may love the lithe and airy forms of wildflowers, you probably should not turn your front yard into a cottage garden. Instead, consider using neat, low-growing annuals.

Also keep in mind the scale of the structures and landscape your annuals will adorn. A three-story Victorian would overpower a wee plot of pansies completely. Conversely, a thicket of elephant's ears will overwhelm a little bungalow. If you put cosmos at the edge of the deck, will you be able to see the lawn?

The dimensions of your yard will dictate annuals of a certain stature. A huge yard will accommodate tall plants easily—in fact, anything smaller than a sunflower may not be seen at all. That doesn't mean, however, that small gardens must be filled only with pint-sized plants. Low-growing annuals can make a small yard seem larger, and tall annuals can lend a feeling of privacy and coziness.

Finally, imagine how your plants will look alongside one another. An attractive flower bed or border combines plants of different shapes, heights, and textures to create pleasing harmonies or contrasts. The traditional English border, for example, combines spiky forms with rounded ones—a reliable formula for nearly every garden. Planting low-growing annuals in front of taller ones, another English border basic, creates a pleasant variety and hides the legginess of taller plants. Height issues can be practical, too: jumbo-sized annuals planted next to knee-high perennials, by summertime will create so much shade that the smaller plants won't grow.

Think also about the forms and textures of your flowers and foliage. Do you want the airy, fernlike leaves of cosmos at the back of your border, or would the more solid foliage of mallow make a better background? Would you like a cloudlike ground cover of love-in-a-mist, or would fleshy-leaved periwinkle be more suitable?

Your home's architecture and your already-existing garden space can help guide your choices, and in turn your annual plantings will adorn them.

# ANNUAL SHAPES, HEIGHTS, AND TEXTURES

*(Left top) Vining plants, including morning glory and scarlet runner bean, are a good choice for covering a shade arbor, a gateway arch, or another overhead structure.*

*(Left bottom) Low-growing plants such as zinnia are diminutive only in size—their color can be vibrant and demanding of full attention.*

*The spectrum of annual flowers includes both the giant and the wee. Each is suited well for use in your garden, be it in a house-high row or spilling from a 4-in. (10-cm) pot.*

## SELECTING HEALTHY PLANTS

*(Right) Look until you find a garden store that has neat, clean aisles filled with healthy, vigorous plants. Pride of display often accompanies thorough garden knowledge upon which you may rely with confidence.*

*(Bottom) The simple act of slipping plants out of their container prior to purchase will reveal whether they are rootbound, recently replanted, or otherwise mistreated.*

When most of us go to the market, we set out with a fair idea of what we need and an instinct about how to evaluate what we're buying. Those same shopping instincts are easily achieved when buying annuals.

In making your shopping list, the first decision is whether to grow your annuals from seed or from nursery starts. Buying seed is less costly, while transplants require little nurturing. In some cases, seeds may be your only choice, especially if you are determined to have the only schizanthus on your block. Are you fond of cosmos? So popular is it—and so quickly does it become unwieldy—that few retailers sell it as a started plant. Do you like larkspur? You won't find it in six-packs next to the flats of pansies because it's one of several annuals that doesn't tolerate transplanting.

In general, bedding plants are the fastest, most convenient way to start your garden. They are your best bet if you haven't got much time to nurture tender sprouts, you're impatient to see some flowers, or you live in a short-season climate. They are your only option if you were late starting your garden and too little time remains for annuals to bloom before the first frost. You'll also want to look for nursery starts if you desire annuals, such as petunias, that can't be grown easily from seeds.

Buying good seeds is about as simple as buying a box of breakfast cereal. Check to see that they're less than a year old—their packing date is stamped on every package—and that they appear to have been stored properly in a dry, cool, airy place. Pass them by if the package is puckered from exposure to moisture or faded as though it's been sitting in the sun.

Buying nursery stock is a little trickier—more akin to picking produce than corn flakes. You'll face an array of choices, from six-packs of seedlings in 1-inch (25-mm) cell packs to mature plants in 1-gallon (3.8-l) containers. Which should you buy?

If it's still early in the season and you can wait eight to ten weeks for your garden to mature, go for cells; if you're starting late, buy larger transplants for instant color, keeping in mind that they will have to be watered very diligently. If you're not sure what variety or cultivar would be best, look for All America Selections, which have been evaluated and chosen by a panel of experts for their outstanding blooms or their vigor and adaptability.

Once you've chosen your prospective plants, you'll want to make sure they're healthy. Plants that were underwatered, undernourished, or grew too large for their pots will be slow to establish themselves in your garden. In most cases, they also will bloom poorly and need constant watering. Look first at where they're displayed: make sure they're not baking in the sun and that their soil is moist. Pick plants that are uniformly shaped, compact, and bushy; avoid any that are spindly, floppy, or listing. Check the foliage, which should look healthy and unpuckered. It should be rich green, not yellow or brown tipped, a sign of improper watering and malnutrition. Leaves should never be mottled, wilted, or brittle. Look underneath the leaves for whiteflies—evidenced by a flurry of tiny white insects— and spider mites, with their telltale tiny webs on stippled foliage. Also inspect the leaves, stems, and shoot tips for sticky residue, a sign of aphids.

Finally, very gently invert and slip the plant out of its container to examine its roots, which should be white, not brown and soft. If the roots are wound into a tight spiral, the specimen is rootbound. You may be able to salvage it, but you'll be better off with a plant that has a rootball with visible soil.

Though it's tempting to buy plants with the biggest blooms, shun them for younger, flowerless ones bearing abundant buds; they will adapt to the garden more readily and are less likely to be rootbound. Be especially wary of plants that are frenetically flowering very early in the season: they may have been forced into bloom before it was safe to set the plants outdoors and likely will suffer severe shock when you transplant them, especially if the weather isn't warm enough. It isn't easy to bypass the prettiest plants in favor of the healthiest ones, but it's like avoiding the candy aisle when what you came to buy was carrots.

*Poor nursery and store care, together with slow-moving stock, can cause plants to be stunted or leggy. The best ones are compact and vigorous, with healthy leaves and well-developed roots. They also should be free of obvious pests and disease.*

**Determining Plant-buying Needs**
How many bedding plants you'll need will depend on what kind you're buying, not on how big they are when you get them. Check Annual Plants and Tender Perennials [see pg. 91] to find out how far apart your chosen annuals should be spaced. Then, using the chart below, multiply the number of plants per square foot (square meters) by the square footage (square meters) of your garden.

| Spacing Between Plants | Plants Per Sq. Ft. (m²) |
|---|---|
| 6 in. (15 cm) . . . . . . . . . . . . . . . . . . . . . . | .4.5/Sq.Ft. (50/m²) |
| 8 in. (20 cm) . . . . . . . . . . . . . . . . . . . . . . | .2.5/Sq.Ft. (25/m²) |
| 10 in. (25 cm) . . . . . . . . . . . . . . . . . . . . . . | .1.7/Sq.Ft. (18/m²) |
| 12 in. (30 cm) . . . . . . . . . . . . . . . . . . . . . . | .1.2/Sq.Ft. (12/m²) |
| 15 in. (40 cm) . . . . . . . . . . . . . . . . . . . . . . | .0.75/Sq.Ft. (8/m²) |
| 18 in. (45 cm) . . . . . . . . . . . . . . . . . . . . . . | .0.5/Sq.Ft. (5/m²) |
| 24 in. (60 cm) . . . . . . . . . . . . . . . . . . . . . . | .0.3/Sq.Ft. (3/m²) |

## SOIL AND FERTILIZING

To apply an old football adage to gardening, good soil isn't everything, it's the only thing. That might overstate the case just a bit, but soil quality, texture, and nutrients can make or break your annual flower garden.

Very few yards have perfect soil. The ideal soil for growing most annuals is slightly acidic, loose enough to allow root growth and to permit good drainage, and compact enough to retain moisture. Most garden soils will miss one or another of these attributes unless it has had organic material added to it on a regular basis.

How can you judge your soil? It's easy. Dig up a spadeful and squeeze it in your hand. If the resulting dirtball slowly crumbles apart when you lightly tap it, you can start digging. More likely, it will either hold its shape like modeling clay—meaning it is too dense—or fall apart and feel as gritty as the beach at low tide—meaning it contains too little organic matter. In either case, your soil needs amending.

Next, determine the acid or alkaline nature of your soil by purchasing a soil test kit or pH meter at your local garden supply center or by sending a soil sample to a lab recommended by your garden retailer or an agricultural extension office. Most annuals will do fine in soil that is between 6.0 and neutral 7.0 on the pH scale. If your soil is too acidic (the pH is below 6.0), you'll need to add some lime and neutral compost; if it's too alkaline (above 7.0), you'll need to add acidic compost, peat moss, or sulfur.

Armed with this information, you can decide how you're going to make a bed for your annuals. For most gardens, amending the soil is relatively easy and will pay off for years to come through easier-to-work beds. If your soil is either too dense or too loose, you may want to make a raised bed: build a box of brick, timber, or stone and fill it with topsoil and compost, or simply spread a 1-foot-high (30-cm) mound of topsoil at your planting site and top it with 6 inches (15 cm) of organic matter.

Amending native soil involves three steps. First, loosen the soil by turning it over with a shovel or a garden fork— if your garden is large, use a rototiller. It's best if the soil is moist but not soggy. If you quickly hit something that feels like rock, that's hardpan,

*(Top right) Gather soil for testing by digging a hole in the bed, then scraping the sample from the side about 10–12 in. (25–30 cm) below the surface. If the bed is large, take samples from several areas.*

*(Bottom) Most garden stores sell test kits that accurately measure pH and nutrients. Their use requires little expertise or special techniques. Electronic meters also are sold to measure soil properties. They are convenient to use but may be less accurate than the slower, reactive tests.*

CONTAINS 40 TESTS

NO-WAT
SOIL TEST KIT FOR LAWNS, FLOWER AND VEGETABLE GARDENS

COMPLETE RESULTS IN 20 MINUTES

and it will require double digging. After you've prepared the ground at least 10 inches (25 cm) deep, work in 2–3 inches (5–8 cm) of compost and some organic fertilizer, then turn the soil again. Rake it smooth and you're ready to plant. Given such a home, your annuals will thrive.

All this being said, annuals are a pretty accommodating bunch, tolerating a wide range of soil conditions. Some, notably wildflowers and self-sowing varieties, will put up with markedly infertile soil, and a few, such as rose periwinkle, actually will do better in poor soil than in a well-cultivated garden bed.

Of course, every annual has unique soil preferences. Celosias, for example, like moist, fertile soil. Globe amaranth and moss rose are perfectly happy in dry, sandy soil. Monkey flower will thrive in wet soil, but larkspur will fair poorly. It will save you time and effort if you choose plants that perform best in conditions that most closely resemble your region's native soil [see Annual Plants and Tender Perennials, pg. 91].

Ultimately, it all depends on your garden's specific soil characteristics, which may limit your choices but not your potential to have a beautiful annuals garden.

*After soil testing has been completed and you know which nutrients and amendments to add, choose from the wide selection available for the task.*

*A frequently overlooked aspect of soil is texture. Good garden soil should contain equal parts of clay, silt, and sand, together with ample organic matter. It is easily worked with hand tools and both drains properly to avoid standing water and retains sufficient moisture and air for plants to thrive. Improve poor soils by adding organic compost.*

## TOOLS AND MATERIALS

When you go looking for tools, you'll face a bewildering assortment of supplies for cultivating and maintaining your garden. If you're unprepared for the experience, you may find yourself asking such questions as: "Do I really need a floating row cover—and what is that, anyway?" With a little planning, you can avoid unneeded purchases and acquire a gardening toolkit that will last a decade or more.

There are a few basic tools for growing annuals you absolutely should own. Start out with these essentials: a shovel, rake, hoe, trowel, and pruning shears. To help prepare the bed, you'll probably want to add a wheelbarrow or garden cart for hauling compost and transporting nursery starts. A sharp square spade will make turning the soil easier. A cultivating tool is useful for loosening the soil and uprooting weeds. You'll also want a watering can to moisten your seeds and seedlings, or a sturdy hose and nozzle.

As your annuals grow you'll use the hoe or cultivator for weeding, the rake for removing light debris, and the pruning shears for deadheading and cutting flowers. An irrigation sprinkler is essential for every stage of preparation and maintenance. Unless you enjoy extensive hand watering, you also may want to add soaker hoses or install an in-ground irrigation system.

Should it matter if a shovel costs less than last night's pizza? In a word, yes. Not only do cheap tools break easily, but your body will not thank you for subjecting it to a handle that splinters and a blade that can't cut through compacted clods of dirt. Instead, look for a steel-tempered shovel with either solid-socket construction—the handle is fastened into a closed metal tube—or solid-strap construction—a tongue extending from the blade screws into the handle. Pruning shears should be sturdy and sharp; the bypass type with two cutting blades makes a cleaner cut in soft stems than

*(Opposite right) A hose-end sprayer is useful for applying liquid and water-soluble fertilizers, along with occasional application of pest and disease control agents.*

*(Bottom) Keep work areas clean and use only fresh materials; safely discard any unused, outdated products. The beginning and end of each season is a good time to take inventory of supplies.*

does the anvil type, with one cutting blade and one flat blade. Be sure to try each tool on for size in the store. Hold them to see if they're comfortable; swing large ones to see if they have the right heft. A shovel should be shoulder height, with a blade small enough so that you can lift the shovel easily when it is loaded with soil. A flat-head rake should reach your nose when held vertically, and the head should be heavy enough to stay in the soil as you drag it. Trowels and pruning shears should rest easily in your hand and not chafe.

Once you're outfitted with a basic toolkit, you can consider some of the more sophisticated tools on the market. Should you get a motorized tiller? Not unless you have a large garden and a steadfast commitment to it. Should you install in-ground sprinklers and bubblers? Ditto. How about a misting wand that attaches to your hose, moisture-retaining gel for your container plantings, kneepads for yourself? All those would be useful.

What about supplies? Should you pick solid, foliar, or liquid fertilizer, organic or inorganic? The short answer is, stick with organic [see Fertilizing Needs, pg. 77]. Do you need fungicides and pesticides? Probably not [see Controlling Pests and Diseases, pg. 81]. By the way, while you don't *need* a floating row cover—a light blanket that protects seedlings from bugs, frost, and excessive heat—it can be useful in getting your flowers off to a good start.

## TOOLS AND MATERIALS FOR PLANTING ANNUALS

**For Preparing the Bed:**
Round-tipped shovel
Spade, with thick top edge (boot tread)
Spading fork (curved tines)
Garden fork (straight tines)
Mattock, if your soil is claylike
Wheelbarrow
Flat-head rake

**For Planting Annuals:**
Trowels, both transplanting and
  multipurpose
Garden cart (or wheelbarrow)
Watering can, for wetting seeds and
  seedlings

**For Maintaining Your Garden:**
Hoe for digging weeds
Lawn rake
Edger
Pruning shears—bypass type
Stakes for tall plants, with ties
Bucket for small tools, etc.

**For Watering:**
Hose, 25 or 50 feet (8 or 15 m), double
  walled or black rubber
Soaker hoses, or a porous soaker hose

**Nice to Have:**
Brass couplers and Y connectors for
  hoses
Timer to turn on water
Drip irrigation components

**For the Gardener:**
Gloves
Hat
Sunscreen

**Nice to Have:**
Kneepads
Clogs
Journal
Sources for plants and supplies

## SOURCES FOR PLANTS AND SUPPLIES

Once you've taken up gardening, plants and supplies for it seem to be everywhere you look—in front of your favorite grocery and hardware stores, on display at your local home center or discount warehouse, in mail catalogs and the electronic marketplace, and of course, at your local nursery and garden retailer.

A reputable garden retailer is the place to go for high-quality merchandise and expert advice. A good nursery or garden store is staffed with well-trained personnel able to answer most questions and provide you with a wide variety of healthy plants, well-made tools, and garden accoutrements, from soil amendments to sun hats. For greengoods, select a place that grows its own plants and can offer a more unusual selection. Top-flight garden stores stock plants that are well adapted to the region, care for them well, and guarantee their performance in your yard.

*(Top) Information is free for the search in the electronic world of online connectivity. Literally thousands of sites exist with detailed information about growing annuals, as well as every other aspect of gardening.*

*(Bottom) Traditional methods work best when heritage flowers yield their seeds. Wait until the pods have thoroughly dried, then gently open and release the seeds. Store them over winter in a sealed jar kept in the refrigerator.*

In the garden department of your home center, you'll find a bounteous supply of pansies, impatiens, and other common bedding plants at reasonable prices; selection is usually limited to the most popular varieties and changes with the seasons. Gardening tools and accessories abound; make sure that everything you buy is well built. You'll get sound advice on such gardening basics as when to plant snapdragons, but it may be more difficult to find someone who can diagnose what's ailing your Transvaal daisies.

Convenience and low prices are the hallmarks of supermarkets and discount warehouses: you can pick up some petunias while you're buying a Cornish hen or shopping for a cell phone. Low prices or weekly sales may tempt you to do just that. Products of good quality are usually stocked, but always exercise care. Be vigilant about the quality of the tools you select, inspect each plant, and find out when new plant shipments arrive so you can get fresh stock before it spends too much time sitting in a display. Relish the good deals you get, but don't expect to find a wide range of choices or professionals to advise you.

If you're a stay-at-home shopper, order your gardening supplies from

catalogs or through the electronic marketplace. Everything, from seeds to sprinkler systems and even bedding plants, can be sent right to your door. In fact, mail-order shopping often is the only way to get unusual or heritage—antique varietal—annuals. The trade-off is that bedding plants often are smaller sized than the ones you purchase at local garden centers and nurseries. Also, seed packets frequently come with little or no information except for the plant name, and though the catalogs offer plant descriptions and growing advice, they're no substitute for flesh-and-blood experts who know your area's climate and growing conditions.

*(Left) A good local nursery, garden center, home store, or other plant supplier is the best place to start when looking for plants or information about them. Rely on knowledgeable store personnel for recommendations suited to your area.*

*(Bottom) Non-traditional markets—fairs, farmer's markets, and arboretum sales— are alternatives to mail-order and other catalog merchants, often with unique plants worthy of attention.*

## ANNUAL PLANNING FLOWCHART

A flowchart is a written checklist that allows you to quickly scan all the major decisions that should be reviewed as you consider a garden project. The one illustrated here specifically deals with the decisions gardeners must make when they undertake planting annual flowers. A few minutes spent with the checklist will ensure you remember each waypoint to a successful project. Refer to the checklist before beginning a new planting—it will save you time and effort, including second trips to the garden store.

**1** **Site Choice Questions:**
Will you plant in beds or containers? If a flower bed, will the planting be a border, an island, a massed planting of a single flower, or another choice?
If a container planting, will it be in moveable pots, windowboxes, hanging containers, raised beds, or a structural container? How much sun does the site receive, and how much natural shade? Is it exposed to wind or rain, or is it sheltered? Does it have easy access for maintenance and is it close to a water source?

## DETERMINING YOUR OBJECTIVES

**2** **Goal Questions:**
What is the purpose of the planting or the effect you wish to achieve? Will the planting create beauty, stand out, or blend in? Will it mask unsightly features such as utility fixtures, or beautify a landscape? Will it function as an added decoration to an existing landscape feature, or stand alone? How much time will planning and designing require? When must the project be finished? How much ongoing care will be required after installation?

## PLANNING FOR THE PROJECT

## ALLOCATING TIME AND SCHEDULING

**3** **Scale Questions:**
How big is the planting, how many plants, and how much time will it require to install? What is the budget, both for expense and for other resources? Will the project require special equipment or additional help to accomplish? Does sufficient time exist to complete the project personally, or should you consider hiring labor or trades to help? Do you have the skills required to complete the work successfully?

**4** **Plant Selection Questions:** What are the growth habits, care needs, and color display features of the plants you will need? Do you seek color from blooms alone, or also from foliage? What foliage textures and leaf forms are desirable? How tall should the plants grow? What color palette should be chosen: primary or pastel? Which tones and hues of color should be included: contrasting or complementary? In the garden store, are the seed racks complete and the greengoods well maintained, healthy, and free of pests? Are plants of appropriate sizes available when you need them, and how wide is the selection? Are prices reasonable, and is expert advice available to help with your choices?

## PREPARING TO PURCHASE ANNUAL PLANTS

## SOIL PREPARATION, MATERIALS, AND TOOLS

**5** **Preparation Questions:** What materials, supplies, tools, and amendments will be required? Has the soil been tested for fertility and pH, or do you have sterile potting soil or planting mix? If a container planting, have suitable containers been chosen and prepared for planting? What fertilizers will be used? Does the soil require texture improvement through adding compost or gypsum? Should you install a fixed irrigation system or perform special construction? Has the bed been prepared to receive plants? Is the soil temperature right for planting? Has danger of frost passed?

## FINDING HELP AND INFORMATION

**6** **Resource and Aid Questions:** Where will you turn for expert advice? Do you have current catalogs, periodicals, and books containing information about the plants and garden techniques you may require? Does your garden retailer have knowledgeable staff able to assist your decisions and answer your questions? Have you identified your U.S.D.A. plant hardiness zone and microclimate? Are you familiar with on-line electronic resources, or do you have access to your agricultural extension agent? Are there gardening classes available through local educators? Are there local experts that broadcast in radio or television media to whom you may turn for answers to questions?

A
nnuals come in such an amazing array of colors, shapes, and sizes that you can use them to produce just about any look you wish. The caveat is that a random collection of annuals can end up looking like the botanical equivalent of a Hawaiian shirt worn with plaid pants. To have a beautiful garden, you need to start with a plan based on a few simple design principles.

There are no ironclad edicts you must obey when you're designing a garden, but there are a handful of guidelines you'll find useful, whether you're a beginning gardener or an old hand. This chapter will give you all the basic information you need to create color schemes, combine different shapes and textures, use plants for their foliage, and pick annuals that will complement nearby landscape and architectural features. In addition to such design fundamentals, there's advice and step-by-step instruction on planting a traditional English border, an area planting, and a windowbox. There's also a complete set of instructions for building a simple potting table.

Once you know how to create pleasing combinations with annuals, your options are unlimited. Try anything you think will look good: annuals are inexpensive, so if you don't like the results, you even can change the design within the same planting season.

**The variety and diversity of annuals make them a perfect choice for any area of your landscape**

# Designing with Color

*Annuals are not only unsurpassed in the range of colors they offer, but in the textures of their foliage. Because the growth habits of annuals are so varied, the combinations for a mass planting such as this one are limitless.*

## USING THE COLOR PALETTE

Color is the first thing most of us notice when we look at a flower. It's also the first aesthetic element to think about when you begin to design your annual garden. What you're aiming for is a mix of hues that enhance one another, avoiding a haphazard collection of colors that compete for the spotlight. By planting your garden with an eye towards a blend, you can be sure that the garden you plan will be neither boring nor have that explosion-in-a-paint-factory effect. There's no prescription for doing this but there are some tried-and-true approaches that can help you come up with eye-catching combinations.

There are three basic strategies for planning a color scheme. Before you choose one, take a look at a color wheel such as the one pictured on the opposite page. The color wheel is a circular arrangement of the rainbow spectrum our eyes see when light passes through a prism. It's anchored by the primary colors—red, yellow, and blue—with the complementary colors found in between, as mixtures of the three primaries. The pure colors of the spectrum are called hues; warm hues center around the orange half of the wheel, cool ones around the blue half. A hue mixed with black is a shade, and a hue mixed with white is a tint. Mixing white with any hue makes it cooler; adding black makes it warmer.

The simplest way to design your garden is to use plants that bloom in various shades and tints of a single hue. A second possibility is to select two or three colors that harmonize—meaning that they are next to each other on the color wheel. A warm combination of red, red-orange, and orange will enliven the solid-green wall of shrubbery at the back of a yard, while a cool one of violet, blue-violet, and blue next to a deck or patio will lend serenity to the area. The most dynamic combination of all is based on a mix of complementary colors—those found across from each other on the color wheel: yellow and purple, orange and blue, red and green, for example—or you can combine primary colors for the same effect.

*Choosing tones from a third of the color palette—here yellow to red strawflowers—guarantees that your flower bed will have a pleasing array of blooms.*

## USING A COLOR WHEEL

Color wheels, readily available at hobby and art stores, are used by artists and designers to visualize the colors they will use for paintings and other projects. Flower gardeners can benefit by planning their pots and beds with color in mind. The wheel presents the primary colors—red, yellow, and blue—interspersed with their complements—orange, green, and violet. The wheel also may be divided into "cool" and "warm" palettes. Follow these easy steps to create a pleasing color combination in a terra-cotta planter filled with annual summer flowers.

**1** Consult the color wheel as you choose flower colors at the garden store. Here, primary red and yellow contrast with violet-blue to create drama and depth.

**2** Arrange the plants, still in their store containers, within the planter until you achieve a pleasing arrangement. Then plant them in potting soil.

**3** The arrangement features tall red snapdragons surrounded by yellow pansies, which contrast with the violet-blue pansies.

Perhaps even more crucial than a compatible color combination is selecting flowers that have similar color intensities, or saturation. The idea is to avoid planting brilliant shades with pale ones. Soft yellow, for example, might be beautiful with baby blue, but a brazen stoplight yellow would be unpleasantly conspicuous in an otherwise pastel planting. On the other hand, vivid shades of purple and crimson might be compatible, even though a glance at the color wheel would not seem to recommend such a combination. When you're deciding how intense to make your color scheme, keep in mind that less-saturated colors tend to fade from sight while bright ones attract the eye. In other words, don't expect flaming-orange blossoms to hide the utility meter—they'll only draw attention to it.

The conditions and dimensions of your yard may suggest a certain color scheme. For example, bright sunlight will bring out the best in bold, warm colors, but will make pastel colors seem washed out. Warm colors appear to advance in the landscape and cool ones appear to recede. Use cool and pastel colors for up-close viewing, since they'll be difficult to see from a distance; if your flowers will be viewed from afar, pick bright-colored annuals. Finally, think about how your annuals will combine with landscape features. Bright red geraniums will stand out against a gray stone wall, while light blue larkspur will blend with it. Both are perfectly fine combinations; the right choice is the one that appeals to you.

*Your choice of color makes a dramatic difference in the appearance of your annual flower plantings, as seen here in four distinctive container groups from each quadrant of the color spectrum: (clockwise from top left) red and red-orange; yellow and orange; pink, rose, and warm violet; and blue, purple, and light and dark violet.*

Abed of zinnias will look attractive while the weather is warm, but the first sign of frost will turn it into a brown heap. If you want a garden that blooms from spring through autumn, plant a variety of annuals that will work like a tag team to give you months of nonstop blossoms. All it takes is a little planning.

The trick is to make sure that some of the plants in your garden are getting ready to bloom just as others are fading. This is a relatively simple matter of following your planting of cool-season annuals with a planting of warm-season varieties, then another cool-season planting, which will last well into autumn [see Spring Annuals, pg. 14, and Summer Annuals, pg. 15].

The easiest way to accomplish successive plantings is to replace spent plants with transplants of later-blooming types. You also can do a series of direct sowings. Make sure that you're sowing or transplanting at the proper time: if you delay planting wallflowers until the weather is hot, they will bloom for only a short time (or not at all); on the other hand, avoid jumping the gun and planting zinnias when the soil is too cold (the seeds may rot in the ground, or the seedlings may be shocked by frost). As a rule, cool-season annuals can be sown a month or so before the last frost in your area, ensuring they'll be well underway by the time you plant warm-season varieties a week or two after the last frost.

If your growing season is short, you can plant annuals a little earlier by putting them in a raised bed, where the soil warms faster. For a truly long-blooming garden, you'll need to start flowers indoors about two months before the last frost date. Though annuals will get a late start in cool northern regions, they will make up for it by flowering quickly and profusely in the long daylight hours.

If you live in a mild-winter climate, you can have flowers year-round. Plant cool-season annuals in autumn for a winter bloom. When they begin to flag, replace them with warm-season annuals followed by a planting of heat-resistant varieties if summers in your region tend to be scorching. As autumn returns, you can renew the cycle by planting cool-season annuals again.

# PLANNING A SEASONAL PROGRESSION OF BLOOMS

*(Left) Springtime blossoms abound against evergreen shrub plantings in front of a brick cottage home.*

*(Below) By mid-summer, the bed has been replanted with blooms that retain the mood of the garden but update the plantings for the season.*

## PLANTING FOR FOLIAGE

*(Top) This coleus variety sports variegated green and red leaves.*

*(Center) Ornamental kale adds an exotic appearance with its multicolored leaves.*

*(Bottom) Dusty miller is one of several silver-foliage annuals.*

Although you're probably planting annuals for their flowers, don't forget about the foliage. Leaves, like flowers, have distinctive colors, forms, and textures that can enhance a well-designed garden, so consider both the blooms and the leaves.

The universe of annual foliage contains hundreds of different greens, as well as purples, whites, reds, yellows, and silvers, not to mention blotches, spots, veins, and stripes. Some plants—coleus, dusty miller, ornamental kale, rex begonias, and fancy-leaved geraniums, to name just a few—are grown primarily or strictly for their colorful leaves. Flamboyant foliage can add boldness to your garden, as long it doesn't clash with companion flowers; red-leaved coleus, for instance, can be stunning in the right company, but you might think twice before combining it with shocking-pink impatiens.

Even green foliage needs to be carefully incorporated into your color scheme. Consider what kind of backdrop the leaves of your plants will make for your flowers: do you want a striking contrast of pale blossoms against dark-green leaves, or would you prefer the more harmonious look that lighter foliage would provide? Keep in mind that some annuals—periwinkle, globe candytuft, and burning bush among them—have foliage that starts out green and turns colors as the seasons change.

Leaf shape can have a tremendous impact on the way your garden looks. Lacy-leaved cosmos will have a distinctly different impact than the stout, broad leaves of sunflowers. When you're choosing a plant, look at the outline of its foliage: is it delicate, solid, or bladelike? Imagine how each foliage form will combine with nearby leaves and flowers, and try to include a variety of shapes for balance and visual interest. In some cases, you'll find that a plant's leaf form is so striking that it actually can dominate an entire planting. Edge your garden with love-in-a-mist, and its cloud of feathery foliage will create an air of informality no matter what else you plant along with it.

Contrasting leaf textures add yet another element to your garden design: the glistening foliage of periwinkle will be a very different foil for your other plants than will the woolly leaves of African daisy. Size matters, too. You'll need to plant a group of golden feverfew to get the full effect of its dainty filigree foliage, but a single 10-foot-tall (3-m) castor bean plant, with its out-sized bronze, green, or red leaves, will announce its presence mightily.

**Red- and Bronze-leaved Plants:**
coleus
dahlia 'Redskin'
canna 'Durban' and 'Wyoming'
*Perilla frutescens*
*Ipomoea batatas* 'Blackie' (black-leafed sweet potato)
lobelia 'Queen Victoria' (prefers partial shade)
*Salvia officinalis* 'Purpurascens' (purple sage)
castor bean
bloodleaf (*Iresine herbstii*)
red orach (*Atriplex hortensis*) varieties and cultivars
*Hibiscus acetosella* 'Red Shield'

## ALL-FOLIAGE GARDENS

Choosing annuals primarily for their foliage display might seem, at first blush, a surprising decision. However, many annuals bear leaves of distinctive color, shape, and texture, and they can create visual effects in flower beds that are truly stunning. Experiment with a single planting following these easy steps:

1 Select a low-growing foreground variety (here, dwarf marigolds were used), with taller background plants (nicotiana) and a distinctive foliage species for the center of the group.

2 While all annuals bear flowers, those prized primarily for their foliage usually have small, insignificant blossoms. Make your foliage selection based on whether you want the leaves to stand out or act as a screen for the base of taller plants.

3 When a satisfactory grouping has been achieved, slip the plants out of their store containers and plant them in the bed, starting at the back.

4 As the front and back flower plantings mature, they will be set off distinctively by the foliage annual in-between them—in this instance, a silver-hued, palmate-leafed dusty miller hybrid.

## MIXING SCALE, FORM, AND TEXTURE

As you're dreaming up a garden plan, picture the finished product in a black-and-white photograph. This visualization will help tell you whether the annuals you have in mind will combine to look like a garden design or just a random collection of plants. Gardens need patterns and balance as well as pleasing color schemes, and that means paying attention to the interplay of sizes, shapes, and textures.

To begin with, make sure your garden displays a sense of proportion. Think about the overall scale of your planting: do you want a garden of heroic scale, or does your space call for a carpet of low-growing species? The answer will depend partly on why you're planting annuals. Do you need a quick-growing hedge, or are you hoping to fill in areas of your perennial border? Next, arrange your selected annuals according to relative size. As a rule, tall plants should go at the back of your border, with shorter ones in front. This arrangement creates a lush look and allows short plants to be seen while hiding the legginess of the taller annuals. Be sure to plant short annuals in large-enough quantities to balance the scale of the tall ones.

The form, or outline, of your plants is a less obvious but equally important factor in the look of your garden. Annuals come in many shapes, from dense, rounded mounds to open, airy sprays. Visualizing your plants as silhouettes will help you combine different shapes for a design that looks purposeful and pleasing. Here again, your goal is to create balance: soften the impact of solid-looking plantings with open, airy plants; pair spiky plants with rounded ones. Keeping in mind that form follows function, allow your landscape and your goals to suggest the plants to be used. To soften the edges of a walkway, plant annuals with a low, mounding form; if you're covering a trellis, fence, or wall, good choices are creeping plants.

Finally, examine the textures of both the flowers and foliage you intend to use. They may be rough or smooth, fuzzy or glossy, wrinkled or frilly. Different textures can be arranged for contrast to great effect.

*Ideal annual borders comprise plants that mix color, form, and texture in a pleasing and eye-catching array. The use of tall, loose foliage from plants such as bachelor's button and annual chrysanthemum offset dense mounds of alyssum and broad-leafed zinnia.*

## BUILDING A BED WITH A MIXED PLANTING

**A**nnuals generally are planted in group settings, with several individual plants of a single species building either an orderly or irregular shape that joins with nearby neighbors. To emphasize the difference, choose plants that have different profiles, growth habits, and foliage texture, as well as complementary flower colors and shapes. An attractive border bed will result if the guidelines demonstrated below are followed:

**1** Starting at the rear of the bed plant the margins, then mark a wedge-shaped area and plant it with a tall blooming annual.

**2** Next, moving to one side and toward the front of the bed, add an oval-shaped swath of plants that will grow to medium height.

**4** A border swath of mounding annuals at the forefront of the bed completes the plantings.

**3** Add a half-oval of low-growing plants still farther forward, spanning the area between the first two groups to unify the three groups into a harmonious whole.

**5** In a few weeks, the plants will begin to fill in their areas, grow taller, and begin to flower. As a plant moves past its prime, replace it with a late-season substitute that has similar growth habits and color.

## PLANNING AREA PLANTINGS

An area planting is the perfect place to create a more carefree look than you might want for a bed or border. Such a garden also is maintenance friendly.

There are a few things to keep in mind when you're designing a large area planting. For instance, you may wish to pick annuals that can be direct sown into your garden, since buying bedding plants in quantity can put strain on the budget.

Choose flowers that aesthetically lend themselves to being planted en masse: a glade of viola and pansies will be more pleasing than an expanse of crested cockscomb.

One easy way to accomplish all of these objectives is to plant wildflowers. They're simple to grow from seed, come in mixes for sun or shade, for attracting butterflies or for cutting, and even for certain heights or color combinations. In addition, they frequently self seed, which means, in certain climates, they'll come up again year after year.

It's almost as simple to select seeds that meet your desired combination of colors, shapes, and sizes, as long as all the plants appreciate the same climate and growing conditions. Even if they don't, you can plan for them to bloom in succession.

Your simplest option for a large area is to plant just one kind of wildflower in quantity. If you want to bathe an area in blue, plant a ground cover of low growers such as Swan River daisy or a sea of knee highs such as cornflower. If you prefer hot colors, choose cool-season clarkia or warm-season four-o'-clock. Where summers are hot and the soil lean and dry, rely on sunset-colored natives such as coreopsis and black-eyed Susan. In mild-winter climates, a fall planting of dainty Dahlberg daisy will provide a winter carpet of gold.

For a more formal look, fill an area with plants that look decidedly cultivated. You can keep your plan simple by planting different types of a single annual species. If you share the Victorians' love of formality, you can mass plant low-growing varieties of your favorite exotic annuals for a neat, clipped appearance.

*(Above) The carefree nature of an area planting is ideally suited to small as well as large settings, especially when they feature irregular margins. It's best to keep such beds simple, often using intermingled groups of only two annuals.*

*(Left) Fences are natural companions to annual borders. Train flowers into mounds as they grow and let them climb the fence to create a profusion of flowers. Choose varieties that complement the color of the fence or stand in stark contrast.*

Designing an annual bed or border is a little like being a composer: you need to consider each aspect of your design—color, time of bloom, scale, form and texture, and foliage—to determine how your plantings will harmonize.

Let's say that you have a border bounded on one side by a structure and you want to fill it with annuals. First, decide on a color scheme. It's best to stick with one to three colors—shades and tints of a single color, complementary colors, or primary colors. Then decide whether you'll be looking for warm- or cool-season annuals, or a combination of both for a progression of blooms. Next, look for plants of varying height. Balance the larger plants in your back border with a quantity of smaller ones in the mid- and front border for a sense of scale and proportion.

Group your plants so that the forms of their flowers and foliage complement each other. If you're aiming for the unstructured effect of an English border, strive for a diversity of forms: rounded shapes with spiky ones, sculptural shapes with airy ones. You might decide to use alternating drifts of plants with similar colors and different shapes. Alternatively, you can compose a sort of floral fugue by repeating patterns at different heights.

You can use these same guidelines to design a freestanding—or island—bed. Planning a bed is a bit trickier than planning a border because it can be seen from every angle. For this reason, you'll want to put your tallest plants in the center and surround them on all sides with shorter ones. As distinct from a border, a bed usually has a regular, or semi-regular, geometric configuration that conveys a more formal feeling that might affect your plant choices.

The basics of good design provide a foundation for unusual and adventurous garden styles as well as traditional ones. The great thing about annuals is that their range of choices and their flexibility provide the perfect medium for nearly any experiment you want to try.

*Strong, contrasting colors are best planted in small beds, as an accent, or in a container to be used as a floral keynote on a patio, deck, or entryway.*

*Use of a single species of flower—in this case pansy— still permits riotous color to dominate foliage in flower beds. Choose hybrids with similar markings and characteristics as the unifying element in such displays, then span the spectrum with as many colors as possible.*

## DESIGNING A TRADITIONAL ENGLISH BORDER

There's a reason the English border is so popular. Like the perfect relationship, it has no rigid boundaries yet has structure. It is organized, yet varied. Most of all, it is adaptable. While an English border always is organized by height, with tall plants in the back descending to short ones in the front, it further requires a flow of only two or three compatible hues, clustered in plantings of three or more, then repeated at intervals throughout the border. Beyond this, it can be created in any climate. Follow these easy steps to create the English look wherever you garden:

**1** Sketch your plan and trial place plants, tall species to the rear and short ones in front.

**2** Define the boundaries of plant groups within the bed using either garden lime or flour. Stand back and envision the planting.

**3** Install the plants, following the sketched design and marked boundaries. Space plants appropriately for each species.

## CONSIDERING ARCHITECTURAL AND LANDSCAPE FEATURES

A floral garden, unlike a painting on a museum wall, is molded by—and gives shape to—its setting. When you're selecting what annuals to plant and where to put them, you have the opportunity to make them an artful part of your landscape.

The most important element of your backdrop, your house, will play the biggest role in determining the annuals you decide to plant. Consider its architectural style. If it's a stately colonial, exotic tropicals like canna and elephant's ear are likely to look out of place, but if it's a Victorian with gingerbread trim, they will be an enhancement. Then study your home's contours. A geometric knot garden would be a poor foil for the softly rounded forms of a desert adobe house, but draping plants would be a nice complement.

A sense of scale is important, too. In general, it's a good idea to keep the scale of your plants proportional to your architecture, so that a humble house isn't dwarfed by plantings of epic proportions, and a grand one doesn't appear to loom above a strip of ankle-high ground cover. The materials that make up your house also affect your choice of plantings. Rough cedar shingles have a less formal look than, say, sawn ones or smooth lap siding, and therefore would make a better showcase for a planting of wildflowers.

Remember, too, to consider the color of your home's exterior in your garden scheme. If your house is green, for example, you might consider variegated or bronze foliage next to it; similarly, an all-white garden will be enhanced beside a rustic deck more than against white stucco walls. These same considerations apply to all the hardscape features in your yard, including walkways, walls, decks, and patios.

In most cases, your annuals will be sharing space with trees, shrubs, and perennials that already have assumed form, texture, and color within your landscape. If your yard contains many rounded shapes, balance them with tall, spiky annuals. The romantic appeal of a gnarled old tree can be garnished by encircling its trunk with black-eyed Susan vine, or surrounded with a ring of sweet-faced pansies beneath its solid form.

Remember as you're planning your color scheme that your trees and perennial plants may not always be green: some will bloom in spring, and some may change color as autumn approaches. Finally, since your annuals are coming to a party that's already in progress, make sure they're not going to disrupt it. Scarlet salvia might invigorate a planting of assertive shrubs, but in a Japanese garden it would become the floral equivalent of a guest who staggers about wearing a lampshade.

*Choosing plantings that complement a home's architectural style is only part of the story. The same considerations apply to outdoor "rooms." In this case, a pink tuberous begonia lends an air of elegance and serenity to a backyard shade cover.*

## PLANTING A WINDOWBOX

Seasonal color can highlight the architectural features of your home, a job tailor-made for annuals. Filling windowboxes with growing flowers takes only a few hours to plan, purchase, and install. Choose annuals that either trail over the edge or mound high up into the window opening, where they appear as though in a frame. Follow these easy steps for a perfect result:

2 If access is limited, install a timed drip irrigation line to each pot.

3 Plant annuals into the containers, using a pair of transplants in each pot—this ensures that there will be no gaps in the floral display if one should fail. Add a whimsical garden decoration, if desired.

1 Measure the dimensions and depth of the windowbox, and purchase weatherproof containers sized to fit snugly inside it.

4 Annuals grow quickly, filling the windowbox with color. Remember that pot plantings should be fertilized every other week throughout the growing season.

Annuals planted alongside a pathway can soften its harsh edges, connect it to its surroundings, and give it a finished look the way a frame "finishes" a picture. A pathway planting may accommodate no more than a single row of flowers, but that often is enough to make it front and center in your yard.

For this reason, when it comes to designing a pathway planting, less is more. Two or three types of annuals are usually plenty when you're working with a space that's no wider than your morning newspaper. Well-designed walkway plantings are as dynamic and distinctive as their bedding counterparts. In fact, you can think of the narrow strip that borders your path as an attenuated annual garden and plan accordingly. One approach would be to apply the same design principles used for a bed of annuals: choose a harmonious or complementary color scheme, put your tallest plants in the middle, and strive for a balance of textures and shapes that take into account the material makeup and configuration of your path. Another tactic is to plan a pathway planting based on the quintessentially simple annual garden: a single-flower mass of color.

Practical considerations are as important as aesthetic ones when you're planning a pathway planting. For example, if your path is narrow and heavily used, edge it with upright plants that will stand aside. Also keep in mind that the surface of a hard pathway absorbs, retains, and radiates heat, which in turn dries out the surrounding soil, and that stones and pavement can leach minerals into the soil. For these reasons, choose your plantings carefully and adjust their care for these special circumstances.

## PLANNING PLANTINGS FOR PATHWAYS

*Pathways in many garden settings are strictly utilitarian, providing nothing more than access. Dress them up by adding tableaux that are as practical as they are inviting. Plant annual flowers and decorative grasses to complete the picture.*

Give annuals
a good start,
whether you
plant seeds or
nursery-grown
transplants in
your garden

# How to
# Plant and
# Grow
# Annuals

One of the most endearing qualities of annuals is that they're familiar. Nearly everyone either has grown or seen a garden of petunias planted in perfectly straight lines that greets spring like a proud military honor guard. While we may cherish such traditional garden schemes, there are many other annuals and just as many other ways to use them.

Do you want to give your newly planted vegetable garden an infusion of color that will anticipate and complement the hues of harvest time? Could your perennials use a little "filling in" before or after their peak bloom? Are you searching for something that will grow in the reflected heat of a swimming pool, in the shade of a tree, or in a container to decorate the living room or to give as a gift? In every case, annuals can do the job.

Like all of us, annuals fare better with a good start in life. In this chapter, you'll find out how to raise your annuals from seeds or nursery-grown seedlings—and how to decide which of these is better in your case. Included are step-by-step instructions for building a potting table to get you started, and for installing a simple, automatic watering system. You'll also learn how to start seeds indoors for later transplanting into either the garden or a container, how to prepare the soil for planting annuals, and how to choose healthy nursery stock from the many varieties available.

Finally, you'll discover a few techniques for hardening seedlings and mulching young transplants. Once your plants are in the ground, read up on all aspects of caring for annuals, including watering, fertilizing, pinching and pruning, and disease and pest control.

*Annual flowers dress up any residence, especially when planted with perennials and shrubs. Their color completes the landscape decor of both permanent planters and in-ground beds.*

## BEFORE PLANTING

The garden season announces itself in myriad ways, from warming breezes that entice trees to bud and bloom to mailboxes stuffed with seed catalogs. Take advantage of the down-time seasons of late autumn, winter, and too-early spring to put your gardening affairs in order.

Start by making sure the tools, equipment, and materials you stored away last season are in good condition and up to another year in the garden. Sharpen shovels, spades, hoes, and cultivators; hone pruning shears; clean, oil and lubricate mechanical tillers and other electrical equipment; and discard broken items. Replace broken handles or worn parts that are beginning to show the ill effects of hard use.

The preplanting season also is an excellent time to undertake projects that would consume time better spent outdoors when the weather warms. Soil too cold for planting still will be receptive to construction of beds, installation of water ponds, and the addition of birdbaths and garden ornaments.

If you are like many others, gardening is a hobby that plans around—or through—all available space: basements, garages, tool sheds, closets, and spare rooms. Organize your pastime by using the off-season to construct a potting table or acquire a weatherproof prebuilt model from your garden retailer.

If growing annuals is a large-scale activity, make sure the potting table is broad enough to bear several pots and trays of nursery starts; however, if your gardening is restricted to a small space, select a more compact table. Open shelving and convenient drawers are useful for storing materials when not in use, as are hanger hooks for trowels, forks, and dibbers.

Planning for the garden season extends your enjoyment of the hobby, and saves work down the line. You'll benefit from your efforts expended in anticipation of the time when sprouts are burgeoning.

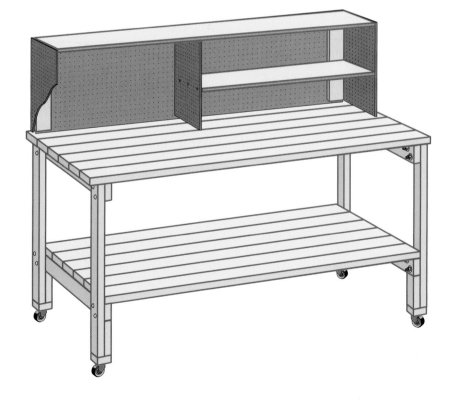

*This easy-to-build potting table is spacious enough for serious gardening, yet portable, and is built from weatherproof pressure-treated lumber.*

## BUILDING A POTTING TABLE

A potting table provides a convenient spot in the garden to transplant seedlings, clean containers, mix fertilizer, and perform other messy outdoor tasks. Many excellent models are offered for purchase at retail stores, but building your own custom table is a perfect winter weekend project.

### Required Materials:

**Pressure-Treated Lumber:**

| | | | |
|---|---|---|---|
| 4 | 30-in. (75 cm) | 2×6 (38×140 mm) | Legs |
| 2 | 31-in. (79 cm) | 2×6 (38×140 mm) | Top crossbraces |
| 2 | 32½-in. (83 cm) | 2×6 (38×140 mm) | Bottom crossbraces |
| 4 | 12-in. (30.5 cm) | 2×6 (38×140 mm) | Crossbrace blocks |
| 4 | 5½-in. (14 cm) | 2×6 (38×140 mm) | Caster mount blocks |
| 6 | 72-in. (183 cm) | 2×6 (38×140 mm) | Top surface planks |
| 2 | 31-in. (79 cm) | 2×6 (38×140 mm) | Top surface supports |
| 4 | 66-in. (168 cm) | 2×6 (38×140 mm) | Bottom shelf planks |

**Lumber:**

| | | | |
|---|---|---|---|
| 1 | 52-in. (132 cm) | 2×4 (38×89 mm) | Front apron support |
| 1 | 66-in. (167.5 cm) | 1×6 (19×140 mm) | Front apron |
| 2 | 22-in. (55 cm) | 1×6 (19×140 mm) | Side aprons |

| | | | |
|---|---|---|---|
| 3 | 18-in. (46 cm) | 2×8 (38×184 mm) | Vertical supports |
| 1 | 72-in. (183 cm) | 1×8 (19×184 mm) | Top shelf |
| 1 | 34⅛-in. (86.5 cm) | 1×8 (19×184 mm) | Middle shelf |

**Pegboard Pressboard Sheet ⅜ in. (10 mm):**

| | | | |
|---|---|---|---|
| 1 | 22×72-in. (56×183cm) | | Top shelf backing |

**Hardware and Materials:**

| | | |
|---|---|---|
| 100 | No. 8×2½-in. (4×65 mm) | Galvanized deck screws |
| 16 | 5/16·×3½-in. (8×85 mm) | Hex bolts, nuts, washers |
| 4 | Caster assemblies with wheel locks and fasteners | |
| 6 | Pegboard hooks | |
| 9 | Vinyl-covered hanger hooks (screw-in) | |
| 1 | Bottle woodworker's exterior glue | |

**1** Cut legs, crossbraces, crossbrace blocks, and caster mount blocks. On a flat work surface, align two legs parallel, 33 in. (84 cm) apart. Flush top crossbrace to top corner of back leg and top of front leg, allowing 1½-in. (38-mm) setback from front leg edge. Align crossbrace blocks parallel and flush to the bottom of each leg, then mark, drill, glue, and attach with four deck screws. Flush bottom crossbrace to outside edge of each leg, tight to the crossbrace block. Square and clamp the assembly, mark and drill two ¼-in. (6-mm) holes at each leg-crossbrace junction. Thread a washer onto each bolt, then drive the bolts through the legs and crossbraces. Attach the final washer and nut on each bolt, then tighten until the wood just compresses. Release the clamps as each joint is secured. Align a caster block at the foot of each leg and attach with four deck screws. Repeat steps for second leg assembly.

**2** Cut top surface planks, top surface supports, and front apron support. Loosely align the six planks, squaring them into a rectangle. Apply glue to each edge of the four central planks, square, clamp tightly, and allow to dry overnight. Measure 4½ in. (11.5 cm) from each of the 33-in. (84-cm) edges of the assembly and draw two lines. Place a work surface support on the inside of each line, flush with the assembly's back edge and 2 in. (50 mm) short of its front edge, and clamp. Drill two ⅛×2-in. (3×50-mm) holes, two to each top plank, through the support and into (but not through) the top planks. Attach supports to the surface assembly with deck screws. Attach the front apron support between the work surface supports with deck screws.

**3** Attach legs: Place the work surface assembly face down on a level surface. Stand each leg assembly on the work surface assembly, aligning each flush with the back edge and parallel and snug to a work surface support. Drill ⅛-in. (3-mm) pilot holes horizontally through the top crossbrace into a work surface support and fasten the leg assembly with deck screws. Repeat for other leg assembly. Attach casters: Drill and install a caster assembly into the bottom of each leg using the hardware supplied with the caster.

**4** Bottom shelf: Cut four bottom shelf planks. Using a circular saw, rip ½ in. (10 mm) off of one plank, making it 5 in. (13 cm) wide. Stand the bench on its legs, check it for square, and place the bottom shelf planks so that they span the bottom crossbraces. Flush each plank to the outer edge of the crossbraces, clamp, and drill two ⅛-in. (3-mm) pilot holes through each plank end into the crossbrace. Fasten with deck screws.

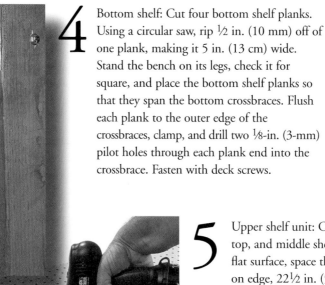

**5** Upper shelf unit: Cut vertical shelf supports, top, and middle shelf. Cut pegboard. On a flat surface, space the shelf supports, parallel on edge, 22½ in. (57 cm) apart. Fit the top shelf to their ends, drill ⅛-in. (3-mm) pilot holes, and fasten the shelf to the supports with three deck screws driven into each support. Measure 8¼ in. (21 cm) from the base of the middle and left shelf supports and mark a line. Align the middle shelf between the two supports with its base on the line. Drill pilot holes, then fasten the shelf to its supports. Square the pegboard to the shelf assembly, overhanging the bottom edge by 4 in. (10 cm). Fasten to supports with deck screws.

**6** Work-shelf aprons: Cut the front and side aprons. Fit the side aprons flush against the top crossbraces, using them as a stop. Drill pilot holes through the aprons and fasten them with deck screws. Fit the front apron onto its apron support, predrill, and fasten it with deck screws.

**7** Attach the shelf unit: Position the shelf assembly atop the work surface, aligned to sides and back. Mark the location of the shelf supports on the work surface, remove the shelf, and drill pilot holes through the work surface, two to each support. Replace the shelf unit. Working from the underside, attach the shelf unit to the work surface with deck screws. Drill equally spaced holes through the pegboard and fasten the overhanging edge with deck screws.

**8** Final assembly: Obtain and install pegboard and vinyl hanger hooks. Drill ¼-in. (6-mm) pilot holes equally spaced in the aprons and attach the vinyl hooks for hand tools. Optional wire-basket assemblies may be attached to the bottom of the lower shelf unit.

## PLANTING SEEDS

Starting annuals from seeds often is your best option and, in some cases, your only one. Uncommon annuals can be difficult to find as started plants, and even if you're in the market for the most popular annuals, you may be hard-pressed to find, say, two dozen pink 'Peter Pan' zinnias in flats. If you want to plant heirloom varieties, seeds likely will be your only choice. Where the growing season is short, starting seeds expands your plant palette to include warm-season annuals that wouldn't have time to mature between first and last frost if sown outdoors.

If you're starting several plants of a given variety, an effective method is to start them in undivided flats, then transplant them to individual containers [see Transplanting into Pots, pg. 63] after they've sprouted. You'll need waterproof trays in which to set your flats, and sterile potting soil mix—never use garden soil, which may harbor diseases. Be sure to read all of the instructions on the seed package before you begin. It usually will tell you whether your seeds need to be chilled or soaked before sowing, what temperature soil they need for germination, how long it will take them to sprout, and how they should be spaced for planting.

Never irrigate seed plantings with a stream of water—it's easy to flood and loosen them from the soil; instead, mist them. Perhaps most important, keep your plantings warm. All seeds need a minimum temperature in their soil for germination and healthy growth. You can keep your covered flats warm by putting them on top of the refrigerator or water heater, or buy a grow mat or heating cable from a garden retailer or catalog. After the package-recommended germination period, start examining your seeds every day for signs of sprouting; most seeds emerge from the soil in one to three weeks.

When first sprouts appear, uncover the flats immediately—allowing air to circulate—and give them a reliable source of light. A sunny windowsill will suffice for growing many common annuals, but a constant source of ultraviolet-rich artificial light is far more effective. Most garden retailers stock so-called "grow-lights," fluorescent tubes that emit a complete spectrum of light. Use them in anything from a tabletop fluorescent fixture to an elaborate propagation station.

*Seeding directly into garden beds is the best method to use for plants that are easily grown or that are difficult to transplant [see Sowing Seeds in Beds, pg. 65]. Check soil temperatures if planting takes place early in the season to avoid damping off, a fungal disease that kills young sprouts by rotting their stems.*

## STARTING ANNUALS FROM SEED

Starting seeds indoors requires a little time but gives you the opportunity to grow heirloom flowers as well as species that require an early start to accommodate a short growing season. If you've never tried starting seeds indoors before, begin with just a few varieties. When you see them all grown up and on their own in the garden, you won't be able to wait until next year. Follow these simple steps for best results:

### Warning

Household bleach contains sodium hypochlorite, a powerful skin and eye irritant. Avoid hazard by wearing gloves and protecting clothing whenever mixing or pouring bleach solution.

**1** Clean tray and tools with a mixture of 1 part household bleach to 9 parts water. Fill tray with potting soil. Open furrows in parallel rows.

**2** Carefully tap seeds from the seed package into each of the prepared rows, spacing the seeds as recommended by the seed supplier.

**3** Close the furrow over each seed, burying the seed to the depth recommended on the package. Press the soil with your palms until it is firm. Good soil contact is essential to germination.

**4** Seedlings are ready for transplant after they have developed two true leaves.

## PLANTING IN CONTAINERS

There are times when you'll want to start seeds in individual pots rather than communal flats, especially if you're starting small numbers of several different annuals. You won't be able to sow as many plants if you opt for individual pot plantings, but the seedlings that result will benefit by having extra vigor.

Start by reading the instructions contained on the seed package or in the catalog. Sow two to three seeds in each pot, setting them to the recommended depth, then proceed with the steps outlined for planting seeds in flats [see Starting Annuals from Seed, pg. 61]. Instead of transplanting your seedlings when they're an inch or two (25–50 mm) high, thin them by using a small pair of scissors to snip off all but the strongest pair of specimens in each pot. You can use your fingers or a pair of tweezers to do this job, but use care to avoid disturbing the surviving seedlings. Give your seedlings adequate water—at least twice a week—and ensure that the soil stays moist. Provide adequate light artificially or naturally, placing the pot under full-spectrum fluorescent lights or on a sunny windowsill.

After hardening your plants [see Hardening Transplants, pg. 66], you'll be able to set them into the ground. If you're working with annuals that tolerate transplanting, you can grow seedlings individually in less-expensive 4-inch (10-cm) plastic pots or cell packs left over from last year's nursery starts. Always sterilize the pots first with a solution of one part household bleach (sodium hypochlorite) and nine parts water, using care to avoid damage to yourself or your clothing [see Warning, pg. 61].

Seedlings grown in individual pots will have an advantage over their flat-planted counterparts. Like siblings sharing a bedroom, seeds that are started in undivided flats experience a good deal of competition early in their lives, making the plants less robust. Plants propagated in individual pots are less likely to succumb to weather changes once they're in the garden. Additionally, disease-related problems are minimized when plantings are segregated in individual containers.

*Always use containers large enough to accommodate the plants' root growth until they are ready for transplant. Remember that roots usually extend into the soil at least the same depth as the height of the plant.*

## TRANSPLANTING INTO POTS

Individual pots are the ideal place for annuals not yet ready for the garden because of late frosts. Follow these steps whenever you transplant into pots:

**1** Plants are ready for transplant when they begin to crowd each other in the tray.

**2** Use a spoon or popsicle stick to gently lift each seedling with soil around the roots.

**3** Fill a pot with sterile potting soil, creating a central depression equal in size to that of the rootball of the plant. Place the plant into the container, then press down the soil to make sure that it is firmly rooted.

**4** Apply ½ teaspoon (2 ml) of 10–10–10 fertilizer to the soil surface. Always measure carefully to avoid risk of over-application and resulting chemical burn.

**5** Immediately water in the fertilizer. Water daily for the first week, then reduce watering to every other day for another week. After two weeks, water whenever soil dries out.

## DIRECT SOWING SEED INTO BEDS

Many annuals are so accommodating that they will grow from seed sown right into the garden. Direct sowing is the simplest method of starting annuals; it's also the best method to use if you want to fill large areas.

Some annuals are commonly started outside because they are quick growing and easy to propagate. Others are best started in the garden because they tend to fail when transplanted. Virtually every kind of annual is suitable for direct sowing, though, as long as it can be planted at the proper time and still have time to bloom before the weather gets too hot or too cold for it to survive.

Though starting seeds in the garden is not a complicated process, it's not foolproof either. Common problems include seeds planted too deeply or too shallowly, being flooded out by rain or overzealous watering, parched by the sun, elbowed out by weeds, or felled by disease caused by too-cold soil or excess moisture. The good news is that you can do much to keep such problems at bay. When everything goes according to plan you get a gorgeous garden with little effort.

Before you begin planting, make sure the soil in your garden is weed free, free of rocks and clods, and smoothly raked. Scattering, or broadcasting, seeds results in a more casual look, but sowing seeds in a pattern helps you distinguish them from weeds when they sprout. To get the best of both worlds, use flour to mark drifts in the soil, then sow seeds in straight lines within each drift. Cover seeds with a light layer of sifted compost or sand, which easily can be penetrated by delicate shoots. Gently press the seeds into the soil with the flat side of a board or hoe to ensure they have good contact with the soil.

Water newly planted seeds very gently with a watering can or a fine spray from the hose. As soon as your seedlings develop true leaves, allow them room to grow by thinning weak sprouts.

*A healthy bed of annual flowers grown from seed will yield plants that reach the same point of development simultaneously, permitting you to time peak blooms to occasions or seasonal events. Consult the seed package or Annual Plants and Tender Perennials [see pg. 91] to determine the amount of time required for plants to mature and bear flowers from the time of planting from seed.*

### QUICK-BLOOMING ANNUALS

| Plant | weeks to bloom |
|---|---|
| Alyssum | 8 |
| Bachelor's button | 10 |
| Calendula | 8 |
| Candytuft | 10 |
| Celosia | 8 |
| Cosmos | 8 |
| Marigold (fast-blooming) | 8 |
| Nasturtium | 6 |
| Nicotiana | 8–10 |
| Annual Phlox | 10 |
| Pink | 6–8 |
| Moss Rose | 8 |
| Salvia | 8–10 |
| Sunflower | 8–10 |
| Zinnia ('Thumbelina') | 8 |

## SOWING SEEDS IN BEDS

Seeding in the garden is the best way to start flower plantings in large beds—and the only way to start some difficult-to-transplant annuals. Prepare the soil before planting; it should be free of all clods, rich with organic matter, and raked smooth and level. Plant at midday, when soil temperatures have peaked, using these easy-to-follow steps:

**1** Scatter seeds over the prepared bed at the recommended spacing. Sift soil over them, pressing firmly to ensure good soil contact.

**2** In a few days, seeds will sprout. The first leaves to emerge are called "seed leaves." Wait until two true leaves develop before thinning, to avoid confusion with weeds.

**3** If some plants are too crowded, thin by removing the weakest members of the planting. If there are bare spots, transplant some of the thinned plants into them to fill out the bed.

## HARDENING TRANSPLANTS

Seedlings raised in a protected environment go into the world unprepared for the hardships that await them. Whether grown in a greenhouse, a garden store, or your home, young annuals live the good life, with perfect light, moisture, and soil, no cold nights, pelting rain, burning sun, or drying wind. Unless they are carefully and gradually weaned from their comfortable existence, the hard knocks of garden living can damage or even kill them.

Hardening is the process of acclimating your plants to life in the garden by gradually exposing them to the elements. Start by leaving them outdoors during the day for a few hours in a shaded, protected place, then bring them inside for the night. Take them out for a little longer every day, exposing them to more sunlight each time. After a week or so, they'll be spending all day outside. At this point, you can leave them out at night as well, but keep them in a sheltered spot and perhaps cover them with a garden blanket for extra protection. Be prepared to bring them inside if the temperature drops below 50°F (10°C), or if torrential rains are expected. After a few days of full-time outdoor living, your newly toughened seedlings will be ready for transplant into the garden's soil.

A cold frame—a low, open-bottomed box with a translucent cover—is another means of completing the hardening process outdoors. First, attach a piece of window screen to the cover so that it will filter out harsh, direct sunlight. Start by leaving the box shaded, then leave it uncovered for a little longer every day, gradually increasing the amount of time your plants spend in the sun. Instead of bringing your seedlings in every night, just close the box. If frost threatens, cover the frame with blankets.

*For their first few days of life outdoors, either place seedlings into a cold frame, or allow them to adjust by setting them in a sheltered spot by day and covering them at night. Avoid coverings that contact foliage, however; condensed moisture will cause leaves to develop fungus and ultimately decay.*

## SETTING TRANSPLANTS INTO THE GARDEN

A quick and easy way to start a garden is with nursery-started transplants. Bedding plants are sold in most garden retail stores and nurseries, as well as in many mass merchandise outlets. During the gardening season, a good selection of fresh plants arrives every week. When you buy your plants, ask if they're ready for transplanting; if not, they'll need a short period of hardening. Prior to planting, put them in a sheltered, shaded place, and water them well. Prepare the bed before planting, and follow these easy instructions:

1 Gently invert the container and, supporting the plant with your fingers around the stem, slide the container from the rootball. Never pull plants by their stems.

2 Loosen matted or encircling roots with your fingers or a hand fork to avoid girdling after planting.

4 Place the plant into the hole, backfill with more compost mix, then compact the soil around the planting by pressing firmly with your fingers and palms. Water immediately after setting it into the soil.

3 Dig a hole twice the diameter and depth of the rootball and amend the soil by adding compost and starter fertilizer according to package instructions.

## INSTALLING AN AUTOMATIC DRIP WATERING SYSTEM

An automatic drip irrigation system conserves water, encourages plants to develop deep roots, and helps prevent disease resulting from overhead watering, all the while saving effort and time. Other watering methods often pour out water so quickly that it runs off, carrying soil nutrients with it. Drip systems deliver water slowly enough for the soil to absorb it, and places the water right where it's needed—at your plants' roots.

Before you decide on all of the components for your system, determine the flow rate of water from your hose bib, or faucet, by using a water pressure meter or timing the number of seconds required for the unrestricted flow to fill a container of known size. To design a drip system for your annuals, start by making a scale drawing of the areas that need watering. Note the distance the tubing will have to travel, how much the elevation changes from your water source to the garden, and whether you'll need special coupling fittings to make turns or branch around trees and other stationary objects.

*Timed drip systems feature a variety of emitters tailored to specific plants. Choose those with flow rates and dispersal patterns suited to your plantings. Emitters are available as simple drippers, full- and part-circle sprayers, bubblers, and misters.*

On your scale drawing, sketch in the emitter lines you'll need, keeping in mind that they should be placed 18 inches (45 cm) apart. Next, calculate and note the distance the tubing will have to run. When the system is installed, except for the emitters, turn on the valve and let water flow through the lines (a practice that should be repeated monthly to clear debris from the lines), then install your emitters. Cap the end of each line with a removable clean-out fitting. Your drip irrigation system is now ready for use.

# A SIMPLE DRIP SYSTEM

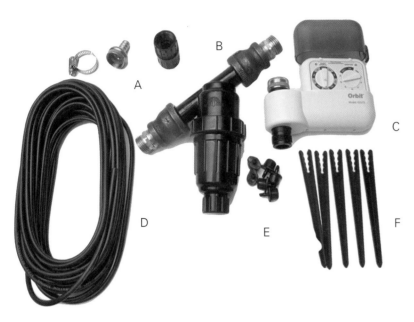

C̶reate drip systems quickly and inexpensively by attaching battery-controlled timers and filters to nearby faucets or hose bibs. Drip irrigation conserves by emitting a flow of water to each plant. A single system can water up to 30 plants, depending on your water pressure. Follow these steps:

Required Components:

- A  Couplers and fittings
- B  Drip-irrigation water filter
- C  Battery-timed hose-bib irrigation valve
- D  Drip-irrigation line hose
- E  Drip emitters
- F  Line-placement stakes

**1** Couple timer valve to hose bib, then install an in-line water filter to prevent clogged lines. Bushings may be needed where threads do not match exactly.

**2** From the filter, attach the drip supply hose. This large-diameter hose carries pressurized water to the attachment points on each of the individual drip lines. It may have several joints and junctions, depending on your garden.

**3** Wherever a drip line is needed, terminate the supply hose with a drip-line coupler, available in 2-, 4-, and 8-connection models. Attach ¼-in. (6-mm) supply tubing and one or more emitters.

## MULCHING

Caring for recent transplants should include cultivating the soil whenever it becomes too compacted and applying mulch to limit weed growth and help the soil retain warmth during times of unseasonably cool temperatures. Organic mulch is best—it provides both good insulation and blocks sunlight from reaching the soil. Breathable mulch cloth and solid plastic sheeting also can be used as a permanent mulch, though they block access to the soil beneath for cultivation purposes. Choose one of the three methods shown:

A Barrier plastic sheet or breathable mulch cloth is applied to the area and held in place with stainless-wire or plastic stakes. Plant through the material by cutting a hole for each plant. Dress the bed with crushed bark.

B Organic compost, pulverized bark, or peat make good mulches for established plantings, especially where soil pH naturally is too high. Apply a layer 1–2 in. (25–50 mm) thick after cultivating.

C Weed-free straw is an ideal mulch for areas that experience short growing seasons marked by cool weather. Apply 3–4 in. (7–10 cm) of straw to insulate the soil, block sunlight, and limit weed-seed germination. When renewing the mulch, remove the old straw and compost it.

## TRANSPLANTING INTO CONTAINERS

**1** Protect the drainage hole from blockage by covering it with screen, then lining the bottom of the pot with coarse sand.

Planting annuals in permanent containers requires care to ensure good results. First, picking the right container is a practical decision as well as an aesthetic one. You can plant annuals in everything from a half-barrel to a wicker basket—the only requirement is that your pot or container have adequate drainage and be waterproof. Inexpensive plastic pots are excellent for retaining water; set them inside a more attractive container if you wish, or dress them up by planting trailing annuals to cover the sides of the pot. Unglazed terra-cotta pots are quite porous, allowing soil to breathe and plant roots to cool; they're a good choice for plants requiring thorough drainage. Overcome the need for frequent watering in terra cotta by painting the inside of your pot with waterproof latex sealant. Still other options are glazed clay pots and thick wooden planters, both of which hold moisture better than unglazed pottery.

**2** Fill the container with sterile planting mix. Choose loose-textured soil containing at least 50 percent inorganic minerals and fillers to avoid compaction.

**4** Plant the container with nursery starts, beginning at the edge of one side and working across the pot. As each is placed into the soil, press firmly around the rootball to ensure good contact. Water immediately after planting, making sure that all of the soil receives moisture.

**3** Add starter fertilizer, according to the package directions. Mix it thoroughly into the soil.

Caring for an annual garden obviously delivers immediate rewards in the form of beautiful flowers. However, so simple are many annuals' needs that the gardening process itself provides the gardener with an equal measure of enjoyment.

Though annuals live only a year, they are hardy and seldom require pampering. They are forgiving of mistreatment, whether from underwatering, lack of cultivating, or limited fertilizing. When you properly care for them, they truly excel.

Far and away the most important aspects of care take place right at the beginning: when you choose a proper location and plant at an appropriate time, you already have a better than even chance of success.

Annuals also are good neighbors to other plants, shrubs, and trees. They generally are shallow rooted (though there are exceptions), and almost any nook or cranny of your yard can support them with ease.

> **Annuals are among the most forgiving of nature's creations, requiring simple care**

# Caring for Annuals

In the next few pages, you'll learn about all the aspects of annuals care, including staking, watering, fertilizing, and pruning as well as how to diagnose and control problems caused by pests and diseases, both viral and fungal, and how to prevent them in the first place.

Annuals are always eager to please; they repay your efforts manyfold with months of color. The hours that you share with them will be marked with beautiful results appreciated by everyone who sees your beds and borders.

*Annuals require simple care, including watering when their soil becomes dry, cultivating to keep their soil loose and workable, and regular inspecting for any disease or pest problems that might occur.*

## SUPPORTING ANNUAL FLOWERS

Tall annuals, along with many smaller ones that bear heavy flowers or sport very slender stems, need support so they remain face up and proud in the garden. The optimum time for staking is at planting time, when you are placing seedlings you have grown yourself or nursery-grown transplants into the ground. Avoid delaying staking; sturdy supports always should be in place by the time the plants have attained a third of their anticipated height.

Supporting annuals is easy. Insert a thin, straight stake into the soil, 5–6 inches (12–15 cm) away from the base of each plant to avoid damaging its roots. You can use bamboo, plastic, wood, galvanized, or powder-coated metal stakes, or any other material that appeals to you, as long as they're sturdy and extend to at least three-quarters of the plant's ultimate height. Sink your stakes deeper for large plants, 8–12 inches (20–30 cm) into the ground, and shallower for smaller plants, 4–6 inches (10–15 cm) deep. Use garden twine or twist ties for lighter plants such as cosmos, garden tape or fabric strips for heavier plants such as sunflowers. Insert your finger between the plant's stem and the tie to ensure you're not tying it too tight. Add ties at intervals as the plant grows.

*Vining annuals, such as dwarf morning glory, require sturdy supports but are easy to train. Lattice panels, sold in many home stores, are easily installed on existing fences or on freestanding posts; use brass or stainless screws for durability.*

Proper watering at the outset is crucial to annuals. Because most have shallow root systems, many will fade quickly—stop growing, quit blooming, or even die—if they receive inadequate, inconsistent, or excessive moisture. Careful observation and a few guidelines will help you determine a watering schedule that's just right.

**WATERING NEEDS**

Watering your plants properly from the moment you sow or transplant them is the most important thing you can do to give them a good start in life. Newly planted annuals need more water than do well-established ones. Transplants may need to be watered daily—even more frequently if the weather is very hot or there's a dry wind blowing. Recently sown seeds may need to be watered twice a day until they germinate; you can cut back to twice a week when your plants have about five true leaves, then to once a week when they are 2–3 inches (5–8 cm) tall.

Well-established annuals need at least an inch (25 mm) of water per week during the growing season, about the amount that a good, soaking rain would provide. The best time to water is when the soil feels dry to the touch, at a depth of 2–3 inches (5–8 cm) beneath the surface (keeping in mind that the roots of some annuals, such as snapdragons, must be allowed to dry out between waterings or they

*Indoor plants have the benefit of limited temperature changes as compared to outdoor plantings, but household air may be less humid than is desirable. At least weekly mist the plants to prevent dried leaf tips.*

may rot). Deep, weekly waterings are far better than shallow, daily ones, which will prevent the root system from reaching deep enough, making a plant vulnerable to drought. Make sure that you supply a full inch (25 mm) of water with each application, or enough to penetrate into the soil at least 6 inches (15 cm). Remember, garden soils vary in their ability to absorb water— depending on soil texture, penetration can take as little as 30 minutes or as long as four hours. Until you discover your garden's rate of absorption, check the penetration of moisture by cultivating the soil a few hours after each watering.

A watering can or a hose with a misting attachment are the best tools for watering newly planted seeds or seedlings (if you use a watering can, twist the rose so that its holes point upward). For mature annuals, use a sprinkler, drip system, or soaker hose—at this point, watering by hand is too time-intensive.

*(Right) Apply water to annual roots beneath the flowers, using a gentle spray.*

*(Below) Reach your hanging plants with a hose-extending water wand.*

Avoid using sprinklers since much moisture is lost to evaporation before reaching your plants; also, overhead watering tends to damage fragile blossoms and, when coupled with cool weather, creates a hospitable environment for diseases such as powdery mildew. Some annuals, such as zinnias, calendulas, and petunias, are

particularly susceptible to fungal disease if their foliage remains wet. If you must water from overhead, always do so in the early morning to allow your plants time to dry before temperatures cool in the evening.

A drip irrigation system delivers water directly to the soil, reducing evaporation, runoff, and problems with wet foliage [see Installing an Automatic Drip Watering System, pg. 68]. It's effective and efficient when compared to hand watering, and though it requires time, money, and labor to install, the system more than makes up for the investment later on. An alternative method of slow irrigation is to use a rubber soaker hose, laced throughout the beds. This system works by oozing water through the porous walls of the hose onto the soil at the base of each plant. Both drip systems and soaker hoses can be hidden beneath a layer of mulch.

Check regularly for signs of dryness in your garden. Yellow or brown leaves, falling buds, buds that fail to bloom, and folding, drooping, or turning foliage are all signs of inadequate moisture. However, they also can be signs of overwatering. If you see these symptoms combined with soggy soil and plants with darkened stems, pull away any mulch around the base of your flowers, let the garden dry out, and cultivate the soil lightly.

*(Below) When watering, apply at least an inch (25 mm) of water at each irrigation. Allow the water to penetrate the soil thoroughly, then permit the soil to dry before watering again.*

*(Above) Overhead watering sometimes is necessary to remove dust or provide needed moisture to leaves, or when applying foliar fertilizers that are absorbed directly through the foliage. Always water early in the day so that the plants will quickly dry as air temperatures climb. All foliage should be dry before nightfall to prevent disease.*

## FERTILIZING NEEDS

Well-composted soil may supply all the nutrients your plants need, but plan on assisting nature through regular feedings with fertilizer. Proper fertilization is particularly important when growing annuals because they need lots of nourishment to sustain a continuous production of flowers.

To flourish and bloom, annuals need three basic nutrients—nitrogen, phosphorus, and potassium—along with small amounts of secondary nutrients and trace elements. The three numbers found prominently displayed on every fertilizer label tell you the percentage by weight of each basic nutrient the product contains. For example, if the package is labeled 10–5–5, the fertilizer contains 10 percent nitrogen, 5 percent phosphorus, and 5 percent potassium. Any fertilizer that provides all three of these nutrients is called "complete." If you're unsure about your soil's needs, use a balanced fertilizer such as 10–10–10, which means it has equal quantities of each ingredient. You also can buy fertilizers that contain secondary nutrients such as calcium and sulfur, or trace elements such as iron and zinc. Fertilizers typically are available in three forms: granular, which can be worked into the soil or dissolved in water; liquid, which is applied during watering; and foliar, which is sprayed directly onto the leaves of the plants (most liquid fertilizers can double as foliar fertilizers). In addition, they are generally available in organic (natural) and synthetic (chemical) forms. Foliar feeding with a water-soluble fertilizer absorbed through the foliage and applied with a hose-end sprayer will give your plants the quickest boost, but avoid applying it in hot weather or it may burn the leaves of your plants, or in unseasonably cool temperatures, when it can encourage fungal disease.

*Use organic compost to provide a gentle, sustained supply of nitrogen and other nutrients to annual flowers. If you choose concentrated synthetic fertilizers, apply them at their label-recommended rates and work them into the soil after application. Always water fertilizer in thoroughly to ensure dilution and limit the potential for chemical burn.*

Plants absorb most of their nutrients from the soil, so your first job is to make sure that you've provided them with a well-conditioned bed amended with compost or other organic material and that you've balanced your soil's pH level (if it's too acidic or too alkaline, plants won't be able to absorb the nutrients they need). Most soils need added nitrogen since it is steadily depleted. Supplementing with phosphorus and potassium, which are more stable in the soil, may or may not be necessary.

It's best to test your garden soil annually. Many reliable kits are sold in garden stores, or you can send a soil sample to a laboratory recommended by your local agricultural extension office. Add missing nutrients and balance pH levels in your soil prior to planting. As you prepare your garden, dig in well-rotted manure and abundant organic compost, along with either lime or sulfur (as your soil's pH needs dictate). An inch or two (25–50 mm) of compost will break down slowly, enriching the soil over time, and also will improve workability and texture. If you're planting annuals between perennials or shrubs, add some compost and a little fertilizer into each planting hole.

Organic fertilizers should be incorporated into garden soil before planting because they release their nutrients with the help of soil bacteria, decomposing slowly and providing nutrients to the plants' roots for weeks or months. Organic fertilizers provide significant environmental benefits: they break down slowly and tend to remain in the soil instead of leaching or washing into local water sources; they also support earthworms and beneficial microbes. Synthetic chemical fertilizers generally are less expensive and more quick acting than organic ones, but they have to be applied more frequently and may burn your annuals. If you decide to use a chemical fertilizer, choose a slow-release version designed to disperse nutrients gradually. Such mixtures may last you the entire season and will avoid some of the environmental problems common to quick-release formulations. Look for a product that has at least half of its nitrogen in slow-release form, and note the temperature required for effectiveness; many do not activate until the soil temperature exceeds 75°F (24°C).

*The right amount of fertilizer is essential—always measure carefully when applying concentrated plant food.*

Even annuals planted in a well-prepared bed should be fertilized every month or two as they grow. Dwindling flowers or yellowing leaves often signal a need for more nitrogen. Always water thoroughly after fertilizing your plants; when the soil is too dry, concentrated fertilizer can burn plant roots.

Finally, keep in mind that too much fertilizer is far worse than none at all for most annuals. Overfertilizing can damage or even kill your flowers, may leave foliage dry and with burned edges, or promote leggy and weak growth. In the case of too much nitrogen, plants will produce lush foliage at the expense of blooms.

Remember also that, occasionally, any fertilizing is too much: if you feed plants such as love-lies-bleeding, spider flower, gazania, nasturtium, and moss rose, you'll end up with no flowers at all. It's a rare annual that requires fertilizing more than once a month—container plants are an exception—but keep in mind that frequent waterings will wash nutrients from the soil. If you're unsure whether to fertilize, take the safest route and simply observe your plants. A dose of fertilizer judiciously applied usually is the best course of action if their growth or flowering seems to be flagging or their foliage color and number of blooms are fading.

## FERTILIZING ANNUALS

Established plantings should be fertilized regularly throughout the growing season (except for varieties that prefer low-nutrient soils). Organic fertilizers, including fish emulsion and compost, are low-yield, slow-release sources of vital nutrients; apply them every two weeks. Concentrated synthetic fertilizers may be applied monthly. Always measure carefully and follow all package label instructions. Choose from either method demonstrated here:

A Measure and mix liquid and water-soluble fertilizers in a clean container, then pour the solution into a watering can for application.

B First, apply concentrates around the "drip line" of the plant—an imaginary circle drawn straight down from the outer foliage to the ground beneath. The finest roots of the plant are concentrated in that area, not near the stem.

Next, work the fertilizer granules into the soil with a hand fork or other cultivating tool. Water the plants immediately after feeding to dilute the concentrate.

## PINCH PRUNING

Nearly every annual benefits from being pinched or pruned throughout its life. Young plants should be pinched back so their growth is bushy and uniform. Later on, spent flowers should be pinched off—deadheaded—to encourage the plants to continue to bloom.

Pinching back young plants causes them to direct their energy into sending out lateral shoots instead of growing tall and rangy. When seedlings are 2–4 inches (5–10 cm) tall, or when transplants are ready to be set in the garden, pinch off the top growth with your thumbnail and index finger. As the plants grow, keep them pruned by pinching off the terminal bud on each branch. Plants that tend to get leggy can be cut or pinched back quite severely and be the better for it. Remove at least a third of each stem for best results, whole branches if they appear ungainly.

Deadheading spent blossoms has two purposes: it keeps your annuals looking neat and increases their output of flowers. Because annuals live for only one season, they are driven genetically to reproduce themselves by setting seed. Until they have accomplished that mission, they will keep trying to set seed by producing more flowers. By deadheading, you disallow their seeds to mature, in essence tricking the plant into blooming longer.

You probably won't deadhead every single annual in your garden. Some, such as impatiens, are "self cleaning," which means they drop their blossoms before they go to seed. Others, such as China asters, simply don't respond to deadheading by producing new flowers; once cut, they're finished blooming for the season. For these, you may want to skip deadheading so you can save seed—either for next season, or to provide food for songbirds.

**1** Pruning is needed whenever your plants bear dead flowers and leggy growth.

**3** Pinch or cut leggy foliage with few buds. This makes the plant more compact and encourages new growth from dormant buds.

**2** Begin by pinching each spent blossom at its junction with the stem.

J ust as someone with a weakened immune system can develop pneumonia after a common cold, plants in poor health are susceptible to pests and disease. Annuals that are underwatered, undernourished, or stressed in any way can succumb to afflictions that wouldn't phase a stronger plant.

The best way to defend against insects and ailments, even before you plant, is to choose disease-resistant varieties, adaptable species, and a diverse assortment of plants that encourage beneficial insects to stay in your garden.

If you're shopping for transplants, check them for signs of diseases and pests [see Selecting Healthy Plants, pg. 28]. Make sure that your planting site suits the plants you've chosen. Rotate annuals through your beds from season to season since soil tends to harbor diseases that destroy repeat plantings. Help eliminate lingering insects and disease-causing organisms by cultivating the soil prior to planting and periodically thereafter. Cultivating exposes organisms to the sun, killing them or limiting their growth.

As you're digging, add enough compost or other organic matter to provide adequate drainage and aeration. This helps eliminate insect hiding places and destroys the fungus that causes damping off, rust, and downy mildew. Avoid overcrowding your plants, which causes poor air circulation and results in powdery mildew or other disease.

## CONTROLLING PESTS AND DISEASES

A floating row cover both protects new seedlings from insects and from temperature changes that can stress and weaken them.

Keep your plants evenly moist and properly fertilized and you'll avoid a host of problems. Spider mites and thrips, for example, thrive on dry, stressed plants. On the other hand, allow soil to dry between irrigations or you'll create a hospitable environment for soilborne fungi.

Spray your plants with a stream of water early in the day to dislodge dust and pests. Promptly remove decayed or diseased plant matter from the garden to prevent

*(Top left) Damage from pest infestation is easily noticed upon inspection. Make every effort to identify the specific pest responsible for the damage before attempting control, then treat with measures specifically tailored to that pest.*

*(Above) Disease conditions usually are caused by fungal spores being splashed onto foliage from contaminated soil, coupled with cool temperatures. They affect foliage and flowers.*

*(Bottom left) Some diseases mimic the appearance of damage from insect pests. Black spot and rust are evidenced on leaves by holes and circular dry spots. Always identify the cause of the problem before treating.*

*(Below) Distinguish disease from care problems—often they bear a superficial resemblance. Fungal disease damage mimics drought.*

it from infecting surrounding plants. Even debris that has fallen from healthy plants should be cleaned out, since slugs, snails, and other pests find it a convenient shelter. Remove all weeds, which weaken plants through competition and provide another haven for pests and diseases. When the weather warms, bolster your anti-pest forces by buying and releasing beneficial insects such as green lacewings, ladybugs, and parasitic, stingless wasps.

Inspect your garden regularly for signs of trouble. Look for discolored or spotted foliage, deformed leaves or flowers, stunted plants, chewed leaves, wilting, and sticky, sooty, or powdery deposits. If you notice any of these symptoms, refer to the chart opposite.

If some of your plants show signs of disease, take quick action to prevent them from infecting healthy companions by removing and destroying any with incurable viral diseases. If common fungal disease is the problem, use applications of soapy water every three days until the fungus subsides. Always make sure that treated foliage has a chance to dry thoroughly before sunset.

Insect pests are another matter. Insect damage can be tricky to diagnose unless you catch the culprit in the act. If you spot such damage, consider first how extensive it is and whether any action needs to be taken at all. Your object is not to rid your garden of every last pest, since the only way to accomplish that means also clearing it of helpful insects. Always start with the least environmentally disruptive remedy. Step up to chemical pesticides only when these methods fail.

When using pesticides, first try botanically derived products that break down quickly and limit harm to the environment. Pyrethrin, which is derived from chrysanthemums, is harmless to humans and quickly kills certain pests, but it also is a broad-spectrum insecticide—it destroys helpful insects as well as harmful ones. Rotenone, another naturally derived, broad-spectrum insecticide made from tropical tubers, is harmful to humans and always should be applied with care.

Whenever you opt for such products, restrict their application only to the infested area. Spray on a wind-free, cool day, wearing a respirator and protective clothing, and strictly follow all label instructions.

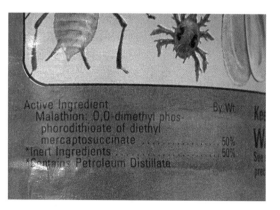

*(Above left) Brown leaf tips may result from underwatering, while yellowing of the entire plant usually is caused by too much water.*

*(Left) Aphids are sucking insects that feed on plant juices. As a first defense, wash them from the plants using soapy water.*

*(Right) Read labels completely and carefully. Strictly follow directions when using controls.*

# IDENTIFYING PESTS, FUNGI, AND DISEASES

| Symptom | Cause | Remedies |
|---|---|---|
| Leaves curled, puckered, or twisted, often with a sticky coating and/or black, sooty appearance. Stunted or deformed blooms on new growth. | Aphids. Look for tiny green-yellow, reddish, brown, or gray wingless insects clustered on buds, shoots, and undersides of leaves. | Spray with hose. Spray with soap solution. Spray with insecticidal soap. Remove and discard plants. |
| Seedlings cut off at ground level. | Cutworms. Look for smooth gray-brown wormlike moth larvae under plant debris or just below soil surface. | Install cardboard collars, e.g., toilet-paper rolls, around plant stems, and sink 2 in. (50 mm) into the soil. |
| Holes in leaves and flowers. Stems may be reduced to skeletons. | Japanese beetles. Look for half-inch-long (12-mm) insects with copper-colored bodies and green heads. | Hand pick. Spray with insecticidal soap near soil. If ineffective, spray insects with pyrethrin or rotenone. |
| Leaves stippled with yellow, may be curled, dry, and withered, with webs on tips and undersides. Plant may be stunted. | Spider mites. Look for reddish, green, or yellow pinhead-sized insects. Prevalent in hot, dry areas. Lantana, hollyhock, verbena, and sweet pea are particularly susceptible. | Spray with water. Spray with soap solution. Spray with insecticidal soap. If ineffective, spray with neem or pyrethrin. |
| Yellow leaves and stunted, sticky plants. When plant is shaken, a cloud of white insects may fly up. | Whiteflies. Look for minuscule white, mothlike insects on undersides of leaves. | Catch with traps. Spray with soap solution. Spray with insecticidal soap. Spray with horticultural oil or neem. If infestation continues, spray with pyrethrin. |
| Off-color, stunted plants. Stems and leaves may have white cottony clusters. | Mealybugs. Look for white oval-shaped insects on leaves, leaf axils, and shoots. | Remove leaves and kill remaining pests with cotton swabs dipped in alcohol. Spray with soap solution. Spray with insecticidal soap. Spray with horticultural oil or neem. |
| Leaves with brown or black spots. Roots and shoots may be deformed. | Plant bugs. Look for greenish-yellow insects ¼ in. (6 mm) long. | Hand pick. Spray with insecticidal soap. If infestation is severe, spray affected areas with pyrethrin or rotenone. |
| Leaves or stems are brown or speckled with white and may be gummy or deformed. | Thrips. Look for tiny yellow or black flies. | Spray with water and release ladybugs. Spray with insecticidal soap. |
| White trails on leaves. Papery yellow or brown blotches on leaves. | Leaf miners. Look for small, pale larvae, and tiny green or black insects. | Release ladybugs or lacewings. Remove infected leaves. Spray with neem. |
| Discolored leaves and plants. Leaves are puckered, curled, or twisted. | Leaf hoppers. Look for small, green wedge-shaped insects. | Spray with soap solution. Trap with sticky traps. Dust with diatomaceous earth. Spray with insecticidal soap. Spray with horticultural oil. |
| Chewed leaves. Silvery slime trails are left on foliage and stems or on the ground nearby. | Slugs and snails. Look under rocks, boards, and other hiding places for adult mollusks. | Hand pick after dark with a flashlight when snails and slugs emerge. Use copper foil barriers around the bases of containers. Set out trays filled with beer. Use commercial baits and gels. |
| Chewed blossoms and petals, especially those with soft, fleshy parts. | Earwigs. Look for brown to black pests with sharp pincers extending from the rear part of their bodies. | Set out crumpled or rolled newspaper—earwigs will hide inside for later collection and destruction. Apply bait or spray with solutions containing sevin. |

Enjoying annuals is easy—just about all you have to do is look at them. Of course, there are many other ways to get even more pleasure out of the plants you grow.

For example, if you've been trying to figure out how to bring your entire annuals garden indoors, you'll find out how to cut and arrange a lasting bouquet, complete with tips on when, how, and why to choose, gather, and place your flowers. You'll also get the basics on growing and harvesting a cutting garden.

On the other hand, if you've always wanted to enjoy your favorite annual on a grander scale, you'll find out how to plant a themed garden, either using several different varieties and shades of your favorite annual or the ultimate—a mass planting of a single flower.

One of the greatest joys of annuals is sharing them—either the experience of planting them or the fruits of your labor. Introducing children to the world of gardening can be one of your greatest shared delights. Because of the simplicity of growing annuals, few types of gardens are as tailor-made for children. By the end of the season, they'll probably be giving you advice about your schizanthus along with proud bouquets.

Finally, you'll learn how to give the gift of color in the form of a potted annual. Make your choices self-seeding varieties, and you've given a gift that can keep on giving.

**Annuals are plants you can appreciate alone, share as an experience with others, or give as a gift**

# Enjoying Annuals

*Flowers from your garden are enjoyed twice when they are cut, brought inside, and arranged into colorful displays for your home.*

## LASTING
## BOUQUETS

When you grow annuals suitable for cutting, you'll rarely need a florist. Nearly any flower that has long stems and lasts in water is good for cutting. For a steady supply of flowers, sow both cool-season and warm-season selections.

Grow flowers for cutting in your regular garden, harvesting them judiciously to avoid leaving gaps in your beds, but if arranging flowers is your primary passion, you'll probably want to plant a garden especially for cutting. When you designate a garden area for cutting plants, try to situate it where a perfect presentation isn't important—depending on your rate of harvest, there will be bald spots here and there when bloom time is in full swing. Remember when planting to leave room for access; you'll need to get in and out just as you would in a vegetable garden.

Confine your harvesting to mornings, when the weather is cool and plants have recovered fully from the previous day's heat. Check for blooms that are just beginning to open, and cut the stems diagonally with clean, sharp pruners or shears. Always immerse the stems of your flowers in a bucket of tepid water immediately after cutting them. This will help condition them, and they'll last longer. When cutting poppies, dahlias, Mexican sunflowers, or other flowers that have stems filled with milky sap, sear the cut ends of each stem with the heat of a candle flame before placing them in water; this will prevent the formation of air locks in the stem that can block the plant's uptake of water.

After you've placed your flowers in water, let them sit in a cool place out of the sun. Several hours later—even overnight—cut the stems again at a 45-degree angle under running water. Before you start arranging your flowers in a vase, remove any low-lying foliage that will end up underwater since decay quickly turns leaves slimy.

*A potting table can double as a flower arrangement station, limiting the mess of cutting and stripping stems to the outdoors.*

## PREPARING FLOWERS FOR LASTING BOUQUETS

The secret of long-lived arrangements is a quick trip from garden to vase. Always carry a bucket full of tepid water when cutting flowers. Immediately immerse the cuttings to refresh the flower, or sear sticky-sap varieties in the heat of a candle flame, then place them in water. Once the flowers have been gathered, follow these steps for easy success:

**1** Recut each stem at a 45° angle to the stem with sharp, clean, bypass pruners. Check that the stems are all of sufficient length and that a variety of lengths exist to give the arrangement a pleasing shape.

**2** Dissolve a packet of floral preservative (available at florist shops) into lukewarm water in a clean vase and mix thoroughly.

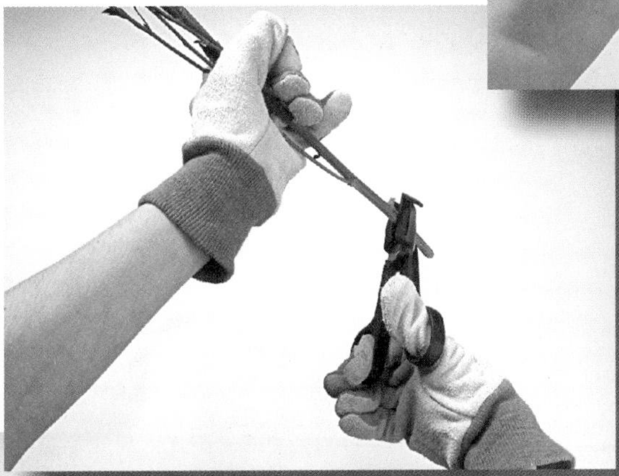

**3** For flowers with woody stems, crush them with floral shears before adding them into the arrangement. This will ensure a good flow of water into the stems and flowers.

**5** Finally, strip away all foliage that would extend below the water level of the vase.

**4** For succulents, such as poppy, sear the cut over a candle flame to prevent wilting.

## PLANNING FOR COLOR

The perfect garden rarely can be seen in a magazine or a neighbor's yard; it's one that evolves from your own preferences and passions. Perhaps you're partial to purple, or maybe you adore sunflowers. Start with your favorite color or plant, build on a theme using a few simple design principles, and the result will be a gorgeous garden that reflects your personality.

You can design an annual garden based on any color that appeals. You might want to fill an entire bed with plants that bloom in darker and lighter shades of a single color, say, pink. To expand on your theme, add colors that harmonize, such as purple, lavender, or other color-wheel neighbors [see Using a Color Wheel, pg. 41]. For a dramatic effect, accent your main color with its complement.

When deciding how to feature your favorite color, keep in mind the location of your garden. If you want to plant yellow flowers near the patio where you eat breakfast, pale-lemon tints will appear to best advantage in the morning light. On the other hand, soft colors become washed out in the bright light of noon; for lunchtime viewing, consider anchoring a boldly colored planting with an intense stoplight-yellow flower. A more-saturated yellow also would be your best choice for a distant part of the yard since warm, bright colors seem to stand out in the landscape while pale or cool ones appear to recede. To tone down a planting of high-voltage colors, soften it by adding some white-flowered plants. If you're among those who like white all by itself, grow a whole bed of such popular annuals as cosmos, petunias, and dahlias; especially when viewed by moonlight, an all-white garden will seem to glow.

*The overall effect of strong colors is less apparent when only a few plants are considered. This may lead to choosing too vibrant a palette at the nursery or garden store for large plantings.*

Once you've settled on a color scheme, draw a scaled sketch of your garden, placing a pleasing array of sizes, shapes, and textures. If you're designing a narrow border beside a wall, fence, hedge, or some other permanent landscape feature, put your tallest plants at the back of the bed and your shortest ones in front. If you have a freestanding flower bed, put the tall annuals in the middle and low growers at either edge. Contrast spiky-shaped flowers with rounded ones, and squat, dense forms with light, airy ones—or repeat similar shapes in different sizes and colors [see Mixing Scale, Form, and Texture, pg. 46]. Remember that foliage and nearby architectural features provide more design variables to consider.

*Build contrast when the landscape features a neutral object—here a gray rock—and choose complementary colors when a precedent already exists in lighting fixtures, walkways, or decor.*

Annuals are perfect plants for a child's garden. They grow lickety-split, scaling their life cycles to the expectations of those who prefer immediate results. Their minimal maintenance schedules are well-suited to short attention spans, and they bloom for a goodly portion of a small gardener's lifetime.

Since annuals come in an array of shapes and sizes, any child is bound to find certain ones fascinating. Some annuals creep along at ground level, where they can be examined easily by the short of stature, and some attain unimaginable heights, exceeding even that of the average dad.

You can make a game of predicting each plant's destiny: which will grow bigger, a sunflower seed or a pansy transplant? Your garden will become such an interesting place that children will return to it daily, all the while learning life lessons—how plants begin, grow, and die; how all living things are dependent upon one another; what it means to be responsible for providing life-sustaining care.

When you're deciding what to put in the garden, favor annuals that are easy to plant, fast growing, and easy to nurture. Big seeds are simplest for small hands to handle; even preschoolers can sow sunflowers and nasturtiums. Older children may enjoy transplanting nursery starts, but they will need advice or help when it comes time to remove plants from their containers [see Transplanting into Containers, pg. 71]. Select plants that are suited to the conditions in your yard so as to avoid disappointment. Space plants with extra room: kids need space to walk among and admire their flowers.

A riot of color may be the outcome, and children probably will find it the epitome of good taste no matter how gaudy. Plenty of easygoing annuals bloom in eye-popping colors that kids will love. You can be sure that tiny gardeners will want to sniff every flower they see, so add at least a few fragrant annuals to the mix, and include some durable, touchable ones.

## PLANTING AN ANNUALS GARDEN WITH A CHILD

*(Left) Gardening is an involving game for children, filled with diminutive tools, bright colors, mysterious plants, and tasks that intrigue and entice.*

*(Below) Time spent with adults in the garden introduces young gardeners to a world that they can create—and one destined to last for a lifetime.*

## THE GIFT OF COLOR

*Assemble gifts from your garden with the particular individual in mind, taking clues from their hobbies, collectibles, or household decor when choosing plants and colors. Remember that the presentation is also important—a gift from your heart is always priceless.*

When you really enjoy something, you want to share it with friends and family. Give the fruits—or rather flowers—of your gardening hobby as gifts, and joy will mark your thoughtfulness.

Container annuals make treasured presents that last for months, and they make ideal holiday gifts. If you're creating a container planting for a particular season, start with a color scheme that matches the occasion. For Thanksgiving, set a container inside a basket and fill it with orange and yellow strawflower. When you're invited to a birthday celebration, offer a pot of petunias laced with silvery foliaged dusty miller. A blue, yellow, and white planting of viola mixed with some hollyhock for contrast and proportion would make an elegant centerpiece for a wedding anniversary [see Transplanting into Containers, pg. 71].

Another idea, appropriate for any dinner party, is to present your host or hostess with a container full of flowering annuals mixed with vegetables or herbs. Underplant red chard with verbena or alyssum or create an entirely edible, all-gold planting of yellow peppers, 'Tangerine Gem' dwarf marigolds, with a cascade of nasturtiums covering the edge of the pot. For a centerpiece that guests can clip and sprinkle over a salad, combine parsley and violet-flowered chives with basil 'Purple Ruffles' and orange calendulas [see Annuals in a Vegetable Garden, pg. 6].

A cut-flower arrangement takes only minutes to assemble and makes a spectacular presentation. Create bouquets of exquisite but challenging-to-grow selections such as annual dahlias, China asters, and lisianthus, or make an equally pleasing arrangement with easy-to-grow flowers such as zinnias and cosmos. In autumn or spring, give cool-weather annuals such as calendulas and snapdragons [see Lasting Bouquets, pg. 86].

Even when the growing season ends, your garden still will supply gifts of annuals. Dry statice, strawflower, and celosia, and arrange them for autumn occasions. Pot up bedding begonias and geraniums from your garden before the first frost strikes and share them as houseplants. When winter comes and your thoughts turn to starting plants indoors, sow an extra flat or two; by spring, you'll have the gift of seedlings to give to gardening friends.

ost annuals are familiar plants and flowers, those seen in nearly every garden. In the pages that follow, you'll be introduced to your old favorites and some new faces, too. There are imports from every area of the world—flower gardening is an international pastime—and growers scout the world for blooms that will excite gardeners. Hundreds more hybrids and varieties are created each year, most destined to remain obscure. Only a few are chosen for propagation and sale.

Annuals come in an ever-changing rainbow of colors. While a few flowers have only a single face, many others range the spectrum and span of hues, permitting you to plant the garden of your dreams.

Each plant has been listed by its most common name, permitting you to quickly find it. This recognizes the desire of most gardeners to look for plants under names they recognize. (For professional horticulturists and botanists, the index at the back of the book contains a cross-referenced listing of all of the common and scientific names for the most popular annuals.)

# Annual Plants and Tender Perennials

Every listing carries the most essential information about the plant—hardiness; classification as annual, tender, or half-hardy perennial; planting, site, and soil requirements; information about care and blooming; tips; and a list of some of the most popular cultivars. Most important, each plant is illustrated in a close-up color photograph that permits you to see the detail of its bloom or foliage features.

The world of annual flowers is a special one. Use this gallery of plants to make your garden unique and noteworthy—truly a reflection of yourself.

**Common name:** Alyssum, Sweet
**Scientific name:** *Lobularia maritima*
**Plant hardiness:** Perennial usually grown as an annual. Zones 2–10.
**Optimal growing region and climate:** Prefers cool weather; not a heat-resistant flower. Ideal temperature: 60–70°F (16–21°C).
**Soil temperature for planting:** 60–70°F (16–21°C). Start indoors about 2 months before last spring frost.
**Soil needs:** Neutral, 7.0 pH, moist, well-drained soil. Fertility: average. Avoid overfeeding; the plant will produce more foliage than flowers.
**Light preference:** Full sun.
**Watering requirement:** Water regularly.
**Spacing and size of plants:** 6 in. (15 cm) apart, to 1 ft. (30 cm) tall.
**Bloom period/season:** Blooms spring to first frost. Blooms year-round in mild-winter climates.
**Tips and uses:** Deadhead to promote further flowering. A favorite for edging, also nice in rock gardens, rock wall niches, and between paving stones. Attracts bees.
**Cultivars:** 'Carpet of Snow,' 'Rosie O'Day,' 'Royal Carpet,' 'Wonderland'

**Common name:** Amaranth, Globe
**Scientific name:** *Gomphrena globosa*
**Plant hardiness:** Tender annual. Zones 3–11.
**Optimal growing region and climate:** Globe Amaranth thrives in warm weather. It is heat, drought, and wind tolerant. Plants grow best in hot climates. A native of India.
**Soil temperature for planting:** 70–85°F (21–29°C). Start seeds indoors 6–8 weeks before the last spring frost and set them out as soon as frost danger has passed. Night temperatures should be above 50°F (10°C) when planted outdoors.
**Soil needs:** Neutral, 7.0 pH, light, well-drained soil. Fertility: rich. Feed lightly.
**Light preference:** Full sun.
**Watering requirement:** Water lightly.
**Spacing and size of plants:** 12 in. (30 cm) apart, to 18 in. (45 cm) tall.
**Bloom period/season:** Blooms summer into autumn.
**Tips and uses:** A long-lasting cut flower, also used in dried arrangements; cut before fully open and hang upside-down in an airy room. Excellent for borders, beds, containers; as edging.
**Cultivars:** 'Buddy,' 'Lavender Lady,' 'Rubra,' 'Strawberry Fields'

**Common name:** Aster, China
**Scientific name:** *Callistephus chinensis*
**Plant hardiness:** Tender annual. Zones 2–10.
**Optimal growing region and climate:** A native of Asia. Prefers warmer weather but also blooms well in cool temperatures.
**Soil temperature for planting:** 60–70°F (16–21°C). Sow seeds directly in garden after frost danger is past. Exercise care when transplanting (avoid disturbing the roots); you'll get flowers earlier if you start seeds indoors and transplant to the garden after nights warm up to above 50°F (10°C).
**Soil needs:** Acid to neutral, 6.5–7.0 pH, moist, cool, well-drained soil. Fertility: rich. Cover with 1 in. (25 mm) of mulch.

**Light preference:** Full sun to light shade.

**Watering requirement:** Water regularly. Soak the soil but leave foliage dry.

**Spacing and size of plants:** 12 in. (30 cm) apart, to 30 in. (75 cm) tall.

**Bloom period, Season:** Flowers early to late summer.

**Tips and uses:** This plant is prone to disease—avoid planting in same location each year. Pinch off faded flowers and yellow foliage to encourage new bloom. Good for beds and containers. Nice cutting flower.

**Cultivars:** 'Dwarf Queen,' 'Giant Perfection,' 'Powerpuff Super Bouquet.'

**Common name:** Baby Blue Eyes

**Scientific name:** *Nemophila menziesii*

**Plant hardiness:** Hardy annual. Zones 2–10.

**Optimal growing region and climate:** Cool-season wildflowers that do best in northern climes and at high altitudes. Also good in both western coastal gardens and coniferous woodlands. Cool, sunny conditions with temperatures as low as 55°F (13°C) are ideal. High heat and humidity will kill plants.

**Soil temperature for planting:** 60°F (16°C). If you seed directly outdoors, do so in early spring as soon as soil can be worked.

**Soil needs:** Acid to neutral, 6.5–7.0 pH, well-drained soil. Fertility: moderately rich with humus supplement.

**Light preference:** Full sun to partial shade.

**Watering requirement:** Water regularly in dry weather, otherwise moderate.

**Spacing and size of plants:** 6–12 in. (15–30 cm) apart, to 12 in. (30 cm) long.

**Bloom period/season:** Spring to frost.

**Tips and uses:** In relatively frost-free areas (zones 9–10), sow seeds in autumn for winter and early-spring blooms. Nice in edgings, wildflower meadows, flower beds, and rock gardens, also in containers, and as a companion planting for spring bulbs.

**Cultivars:** 'Alba,' 'Cramboides,' 'Margarita,' 'Pennie Black,' 'Snowstorm'

**Common name:** Baby's Breath

**Scientific name:** *Gypsophila elegans*

**Plant hardiness:** Hardy annual. Zones 3–9.

**Optimal growing region and climate:** Prefers a cooler climate. Is drought tolerant once established. Ideal outdoor temperature: 70–80°F (21–27°C). Native to Eastern Europe.

**Soil temperature for planting:** 70°F (21°C). Sow seeds directly into garden after frost danger has passed. If you want earlier blooms, start seeds indoors 4–5 weeks before the last frost date.

**Soil needs:** Neutral to alkaline, 7.0–7.5 pH, well-drained soil. Fertility: average. Add compost or manure to produce stronger flowers. Will tolerate poor soils.

**Light preference:** Full sun.

**Watering requirement:** Water sparingly. Allow the soil to dry out between waterings.

**Spacing and size of plants:** 12–18 in. (30–45 cm) apart, to 8–20-in. (20–50 cm) tall.

**Bloom period/season:** Early summer. Successive sowings will prolong the blooming period.

**Tips and uses:** Great for flower arrangements and in borders and containers. Also works well in rock gardens and wall niches. Pull up the plants as soon as flowers fade.

**Cultivars:** 'Carmina,' 'Covent Garden,' 'Grandiflora Alba,' 'Kermesina,' 'Purpurea,' 'Rosea'

**Common name:** Bachelor's Button, Cornflower, or Bluebottle
**Scientific name:** *Centaurea cyanus*
**Plant hardiness:** Hardy annual. Zones 3–9.
**Optimal growing region and climate:** Likes a warm growing season; ideal temperature 60–70°F (16–21°C). Southern European native. Tolerates mild frost and drought.
**Soil temperature for planting:** 60°F (16°C). Seedlings do not transplant well; best to sow directly into the garden as soon as soil warms, around mid-spring. An autumn seeding in any zone will also lead to an early spring bloom.
**Soil needs:** Neutral, 7.0 pH, well-drained, loamy soil. Plants tolerate poor soil. Fertility: average.
**Light preference:** Full sun.
**Watering requirement:** Water regularly.
**Spacing and size of plants:** 8–12 in.(20–30 cm) apart, to 2 ft. (60 cm) tall.
**Bloom period/season:** Flowers early summer to autumn frost. Successive sowings will provide a continuous bloom.
**Tips and uses:** Remove faded blossoms to encourage further flowering. A good plant for window-boxes and containers. Excellent in wildflower mixes, beds, and borders.
**Cultivars:** 'Alba,' 'Blue Diadem,' 'Blue Midget,' 'Jubilee Gem,' 'Polka Dot'

**Common name:** Begonia, Wax
**Scientific name:** *Begonia* X *semperflorens-cultorum*
**Plant hardiness:** Perennial often grown as half-hardy annual. Zones 2–11.
**Optimal growing region and climate:** Prefers warm weather. Ideal outdoor growing temperature: 65–75°F (18–24°C).
**Soil temperature for planting:** 70–75°F (20–24°C). Plant outdoors only after all frost danger has passed.
**Soil needs:** Neutral, 7.0 pH, well-drained soil. Soil should be fertile; amend with organic matter such as peat moss or garden compost.
**Light preference:** Partial sun to shade.
**Watering requirement:** Water frequently.
**Spacing and size of plants:** 8–10 in. (20–25 cm) apart, to 12 in. (30 cm) tall.
**Bloom period/season:** Late spring until frost. Blooms continuously throughout the summer.
**Tips and uses:** Feed begonias frequently. They are great in window-boxes, hanging baskets, and borders. Lift bedded begonias in the autumn and pot as houseplants.
**Cultivars:** 'Calla Queen,' 'Cocktail,' 'Danicas,' 'Glamour'

**Common name:** Bells of Ireland, Molucca Balm, or Shellflower
**Scientific name:** *Moluccella laevis*
**Plant hardiness:** Half-hardy annual. Zones 2–10.
**Optimal growing region and climate:** Cool weather is preferred for this Asian native.
**Soil temperature for planting:** 70–85°F (21–29°C). Difficult to transplant; if seeds are sown directly outdoors, they should be placed after last frost but while the ground and weather are still cool.

**Soil needs:** Neutral, 7.0 pH, well-drained soil. Fertility: average, but will tolerate poor soil.

**Light preference:** Full sun to light shade.

**Watering requirement:** Keep soil moist.

**Spacing and size of plants:** 9 in. (23 cm) apart, to 3 ft. (90 cm) tall.

**Bloom period/season:** Flowers appear mid-summer to frost.

**Tips and uses:** Pick off flower stems to keep bloom active. Self sows. Good drying flower.

**Cultivars:** Not sold by varietal name.

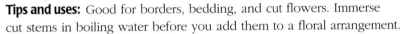

**Common name:** Black-eyed Susan

**Scientific name:** *Rudbeckia hirta*

**Plant hardiness:** Half-hardy annual, biennial, or short-lived perennial. Zones 3–10.

**Optimal growing region and climate:** 70–75°F (21–24°C) ideal outdoor temperature. Prefers warm weather and is drought and heat resistant.

**Soil temperature for planting:** 65–70°F (18–21°C). Sow outdoors in warm soil or start seeds indoors 8–10 weeks before the last frost.

**Soil needs:** Neutral, 7.0 pH, well-drained soil. Fertility: average. Tolerates poor soil.

**Light preference:** Full sun.

**Watering requirement:** Water regularly.

**Spacing and size of plants:** 1–2 ft. (30–60 cm) apart, to 3 ft. (90 cm) tall.

**Bloom period/season:** Mid-summer to autumn.

**Tips and uses:** Good for borders, bedding, and cut flowers. Immerse cut stems in boiling water before you add them to a floral arrangement.

**Cultivars:** 'Double Gloriosa Daisy,' 'Double Gold,' 'Gloriosa Daisy,' 'Irish Eyes,' 'Pinwheel,' 'Single Mixed'

**Common name:** Black-eyed Susan Vine

**Scientific name:** *Thunbergia alata*

**Plant hardiness:** Tender annual. Zones 7–10.

**Optimal growing region and climate:** Prefers a warmer clime. Ideal temperature range: 65–75°F (18–24°C). Asiatic and African origin.

**Soil temperature for planting:** 70–85°F (21–29°C). In colder climates, start indoors 6–8 weeks before last frost, otherwise sow seeds in garden early to late spring when ground is warm.

**Soil needs:** Neutral, 7.0 pH, moist, loamy, and well-drained soil. Fertility: rich.

**Light preference:** Full sun to partial shade.

**Watering requirement:** Give plenty of water during growing period.

**Spacing and size of plants:** 12 in. (30 cm) apart, to 10 ft. (3-m) tall.

**Bloom period/season:** Summer through autumn blooms.

**Tips and uses:** When vines become scraggly, cut them off at soil level to generate fresh growth. Can be grown indoors. Used for trellises, fencing, and supports.

**Cultivars:** 'Alba,' 'Angel Wings,' 'Aurantiaca,' 'Bakerii,' 'Susie Mix,' 'T. Gregorii'

**Common name:** Blanket Flower

**Scientific name:** *Gaillardia pulchella*

**Plant hardiness:** Tender annual. Zones 3–10.

**Optimal growing region and climate:** Prefers warm weather and is tolerant of heat and drought. Ideal outdoor temperature: 70°F (21°C).
**Soil temperature for planting:** 70–85°F (21–29°C). Early spring is the most common planting time. In autumn where winters are mild, seeds can be sown outside.
**Soil needs:** Neutral, 7.0 pH, well-drained, light soil. Fertility: rich.
**Light preference:** Full sun.
**Watering requirement:** Water lightly; grows well in dry soil.
**Spacing and size of plants:** 10–12 in.(25–30 cm) apart, to 2 ft. (60 cm) tall.
**Bloom period/season:** Late spring through first frost.
**Tips and uses:** Deadhead to encourage continued bloom on this fast-growing plant. Good in beds and borders and as a cut flower. Nice container addition.
**Cultivars:** 'Gaiety Mixed Colors,' 'Indian Blanket,' 'Indian Chief,' 'Lorenziana,' 'Red Giant,' 'Red Plume,' 'Yellow Sun'

**Common name:** Bluebonnet, Texas; or Lupine
**Scientific name:** *Lupinus texensis*
**Plant hardiness:** Hardy annual. Zones 3–10.
**Optimal growing region and climate:** The state flower of Texas is a North American native that grows easily throughout the U.S. and Canada. Not a heat- or drought-resistant plant; prefers cool weather. Thrives in regions with cool springs and summers.
**Soil temperature for planting:** 55–65°F (13–18°C). Transplant to the garden in the spring after danger of frost has passed.
**Soil needs:** Acid to neutral, 6.5–7.0 pH, well-drained, sandy soil. Fertility: rich. Enrich soil with compost or manure.
**Light preference:** Full sun to light shade.
**Watering requirement:** Water regularly and amply.
**Spacing and size of plants:** 4–5 in. (10–12 cm) apart, to 12 in. (30 cm) tall.
**Bloom period/season:** Short blossoming season, late spring to early summer.
**Tips and uses:** Makes a nice cut flower. Deadhead to maintain vigor.
**Cultivars:** Not sold by variety names.

**Common name:** Butterfly Flower or Poor Man's Orchid
**Scientific name:** *Schizanthus pinnatus*
**Plant hardiness:** Half-hardy annual. Zones 3–10.
**Optimal growing region and climate:** Does best in areas with mild winters and cool summers. Ideal outdoor temperature: 60–75°F (16–24°C).
**Soil temperature for planting:** 60–70°F (16–21°C). In zones 3–8, start seed indoors 6–8 weeks before last frost. In zones 9–10, plant outdoors at any time.
**Soil needs:** Neutral, 7.0 pH, moist, well-drained soil. Fertility: rich. Use loose, loamy soil enriched with organic material.
**Light preference:** Full sun to light shade.
**Watering requirement:** Moderate watering needs, but keep soil moist.
**Spacing and size of plants:** 12 in. (30 cm) apart, to 24 in. (60 cm) tall.

**Bloom period/season:** Flowers from late summer to first frost. Bloom season is short.

**Tips and uses:** Sow outdoors every 2 weeks (for about 6 weeks) to extend the flowering time. Good for use in bedding, edging, borders, and containers; also makes a good cut flower.

**Cultivars:** 'Angel Wings,' 'Candidissimus,' 'Carmineus,' 'Disco,' 'Excelsior,' 'Grandifloris,' 'Hit Parade,' 'Lilacinnus,' 'Roseus,' 'Star Parade'

**Common name:** Calliopsis or Coreopsis
**Scientific name:** *Coreopsis tinctoria*
**Plant hardiness:** Hardy annual. Zones 4–9.
**Optimal growing region and climate:** Tolerant of heat and drought. A native of the eastern U.S.
**Soil temperature for planting:** 70°F (21°C). Sow seeds outdoors in early spring. Sow again in warmer climates during late summer and autumn for winter and spring flowers.
**Soil needs:** Acid, neutral, or alkaline, 6.5–7.5 pH, well-drained soil. Fertility: average.
**Light preference:** Full sun.
**Watering requirement:** Plants require good drainage; don't overwater.
**Spacing and size of plants:** 6–8 in. (15–20 cm) apart, to 24 in. (60 cm) tall.
**Tips and uses:** Excellent cutting flowers. Stake taller plants for support.
**Cultivars:** 'Carmen,' 'Double Flower,' 'Mardi Gras Dwarf,' 'Tall Mixed Colors,' 'Zagreb'

**Common name:** Candytuft, Globe
**Scientific name:** *Iberis umbellata*
**Plant hardiness:** Hardy annual. Zones 3–10.
**Optimal growing region and climate:** Tolerates dry conditions very well. Ideal outdoor temperature: 70–85°F (21–29°C). A native of Spain.
**Soil temperature for planting:** 60°F (16°C). Sow directly in garden after frost danger has passed. Otherwise, start seeds 6–8 weeks indoors before the last frost.
**Soil needs:** Neutral, 7.0 pH, well-drained soil. Fertility: moderately rich. Does well in most soils.
**Light preference:** Full sun to light shade.
**Watering requirement:** Water to establish plants, lightly thereafter.
**Spacing and size of plants:** 12–15 in. (30–38 cm) apart, to 24 in. (60 cm) tall.
**Bloom period/season:** Late spring to autumn. Successive sowings through mid-summer will extend the blooming period.
**Tips and uses:** Shear off old flower stems to encourage new growth. This is a good city plant, tolerant of relatively harsh conditions. Also does well planted with spring bulbs, and for beds, borders, and rock gardens.
**Cultivars:** 'Fairy Mixed,' 'Flash Mixed,' 'White Pinnacle'

**Common name:** Carnation, Pink; or China Pink
**Scientific name:** *Dianthus chinensis*
**Plant hardiness:** Half-hardy annual, biennial, or short-lived perennial. Zones 5–10.
**Optimal growing region and climate:** Plants prefer cooler weather to bloom best. A native of China. Ideal outdoor temperature: 60–70°F (16–21°C).

**Soil temperature for planting:** 70°F (21°C). In mild climates, seeds can be sown outdoors in the autumn. For earliest blooms, start seeds indoors about 2 months before last frost and transplant when danger of frost has passed.

**Soil needs:** Neutral to alkaline, 7.0–7.5 pH, well-drained soil. Add lime to acidic soils. Fertility: rich. Use diluted liquid fertilizer to avoid tip burn on leaves.

**Light preference:** Full sun.

**Watering requirement:** Water sparingly each week unless the weather is very dry.

**Spacing and size of plants:** 6–12 in. (15–30 cm) apart, to 6–30 in. (15–75 cm) tall.

**Bloom period/season:** Late spring to early summer blooms.

**Tips and uses:** Popular in rock gardens and as cuttings. Also works as a mass planting in beds, borders, edgings, and containers.

**Cultivars:** 'Dwarf Fragrance Mixed,' 'Pink Flash,' 'Strawberry Parfait,' 'Telstar Picotee'

**Common name:** Castor Bean or Castor Oil Plant
**Scientific name:** *Ricinus communis*
**Plant hardiness:** Tender annual. Zones 3–11.
**Optimal growing region and climate:** Widespread in the tropics and subtropics. Prefers warm weather. Tolerates dry conditions. Native to tropical Africa.

**Warning**

Handle castor bean seeds and juice with caution due to hazard from poisoning and allergic reactions.

**Soil temperature for planting:** 70–75°F (21–24°C). Soak seeds overnight before planting. Sow outdoors when soil is warm. Best in areas sheltered from wind. In areas with short summers, start seeds indoors 6–8 weeks before the last spring frost.

**Soil needs:** Neutral, 7.0 pH, moist, well-drained soil. Will tolerate poor soils. Fertility: rich. Fertile soil will promote the best growth.

**Light preference:** Full sun.

**Watering requirement:** Water regularly; keep the soil moist.

**Spacing and size of plants:** 4–6 ft. (1.2–1.8 m) apart, to 15 ft. (4.6 m) tall.

**Bloom period/season:** Summer to frost. In frost-free areas such as Florida, they have naturalized.

**Tips and Uses:** If you have a garden prone to pests, this is a good pest companion planting due to its poisonous sap. It makes a beautiful highlight plant for beds and borders and can be planted in containers for a deck or patio.

**Cultivars:** 'Borboniensis,' 'Gibsonii,' 'Major,' 'Mizuma' (compact), 'Red Spire,' 'Scarlet Queen,' 'Zanzibarensis Enormis,' 'Zanzibarensis Viridis'

**Common name:** Chrysanthemum, Annual
**Scientific name:** *Chrysanthemum multicaule*
**Plant hardiness:** Hardy to half-hardy annual. Zones 4–10.
**Optimal growing region and climate:** Prefers a cool growing season and low humidity. The chrysanthemum has been cultivated for more than 3,000 years in China and Japan.

**Soil temperature for planting:** 60–70°F (16–21°C). Sow in ground during the spring when the ground can be worked. Sow again after mid-summer to keep blooms coming.

**Soil needs:** Neutral, 7.0 pH, well-drained soil. Fertility: moderate to rich. Enrich soil with compost or manure.

**Light preference:** Full sun to partial shade if heat is intense.

**Watering requirement:** Water frequently.

**Spacing and size of plants:** 1–2 ft. (30–60 cm) apart, to 12 in. (30 cm) tall.

**Bloom period/season:** Flowers all summer.

**Tips and uses:** Pinch plants when in early growth to encourage sideways branching; pinch again in early to mid-summer to maintain cushiony appearance. A long-lasting cut flower. Also does well in hanging baskets and containers, as a ground cover, and in rock gardens.

**Cultivars:** 'Autumn Glory,' 'Primrose Gem,' 'Rainbow Mixed Colors,' 'Yellow Buttons'

**Common name:** Clarkia or Godetia

**Scientific name:** *Clarkia amoena*

**Plant hardiness:** Hardy annual. Zones 2–10.

**Optimal growing region and climate:** Thrives in mountainous areas of the West. Does well in coastal California as well as the Pacific Northwest and British Columbia. A native of western North America. Ideal outdoor temperature: 60–70°F (16–21°C).

**Soil temperature for planting:** 60°F (16°C). Avoid transplanting. In mild-winter areas, sow seed summer through autumn. In colder regions, sow as soon as the soil can be worked.

**Soil needs:** Neutral, 7.0 pH, well-drained, dry, sandy soil. Fertility: average. Plant does well in poor soils. Feed lightly in the spring.

**Light preference:** Full sun to light shade.

**Watering requirement:** Once established, needs watering only when dry, but keep moist in the early growth stages.

**Spacing and size of plants:** 8–10 in. (20–25 cm) apart, to 3 ft. (90 cm) tall.

**Bloom period/season:** Spring to early summer. Best blooms occur early in the summer under cool, sunny conditions.

**Tips and uses:** Pinch out growing tips to encourage bushier growth. Good for beds, borders, and rock gardens. Will naturalize in a meadow.

**Cultivars:** 'Dwarf Mixed Colors,' 'Tall Mixed Colors'

**Common name:** Cockscomb, Crested; or Plumed Celosia

**Scientific name:** *Celosia cristata*

**Plant hardiness:** Tender annual. Zones 2–11.

**Optimal growing region and climate:** Thrives in heat; does best in a warm climate. Also drought tolerant. Native to Africa and warm regions of the U.S.

**Soil temperature for planting:** 70–85°F (21–29°C). As soil warms, it is best to sow seeds directly into the garden in spring.

**Soil needs:** Neutral, 7.0 pH, moist, well-drained soil. Fertility: moderately rich. Enrich with organic matter. Tolerates poor soils.

**Light preference:** Full sun.

**Watering requirement:** Water moderately.

**Spacing and size of plants:** 9–12 in. (22–30 cm) apart, to 16 in. (40 cm) tall.

**Bloom period/season:** Flowers in the summer to frost.

**Tips and uses:** Deadhead flowers to assure they will bloom till the autumn frost. Nice when dried for a winter bouquet. Good for containers, edgings, borders, bedding, and as a cut flower.
**Cultivars:** 'Dwarf Fairy Fountains,' 'Intermediate Apricot Brandy,' 'Intermediate Red Fox,' 'Tall Forest Fire Improved'

**Common name:** Coleus, Garden; or Flame Nettle
**Scientific name:** *Coleus* × *hybridus*
**Plant hardiness:** Tender annual. Zones 2–11.
**Optimal growing region and climate:** Prefers warm weather and is sun tolerant but winter hardy only in zones 10–11.
**Soil temperature for planting:** 70–85°F (21–29°C). Plant directly outdoors after the last frost.
**Soil needs:** Neutral to alkaline, 7.0–7.5 pH, moist, well-drained soil. Fertility: rich. Feed occasionally throughout the season with liquid plant food.
**Light preference:** Full sun is fine, but partial shade brings out the best colors.
**Watering requirement:** Keep soil moist with regular waterings.
**Spacing and size of plants:** 10–12 in. (25–30 cm) apart, to 24 in. (60 cm) tall.
**Bloom period/season:** Spring to autumn. Can be brought indoors during winter.
**Tips and uses:** Coleus flowers are unattractive—this plant is grown for its lively foliage. Pinch off blooms and growing shoots of young plants to encourage bushiness. Good for beddings, borders, or containers.
**Cultivars:** 'Carefree,' 'Fijis,' 'Fringed Leaf,' 'Rainbow Series,' 'Saber'

**Common name:** Cosmos
**Scientific name:** *Cosmos bipinnatus* and *C. sulphureus*
**Plant hardiness:** Tender annual. Zones 2–11.
**Optimal growing region and climate:** This Mexican native prefers warmer weather and is heat resistant.
**Soil temperature for planting:** 70–85°F (21–29°C). Sow seeds outdoors after the last frost or start indoors 6 weeks before the last frost date. Easy to transplant.
**Soil needs:** Neutral to alkaline, 7.0–7.5 pH, well-drained to dry soil. Fertility: average to poor. Avoid fertilizing during the season.
**Light preference:** Full sun; will tolerate partial shade.
**Watering requirement:** Very light and infrequent.
**Spacing and size of plants:** 12 in. (30 cm) apart, grows to 10 ft. (3 m) tall.
**Bloom period/season:** Late spring to early autumn.
**Tips and uses:** Stake these tall flowers to keep them upright in the wind. Deadhead to prolong flowering. A generally pest- and disease-free plant. Good for the back of border gardens; makes lovely cutting flowers.
**Cultivars:** 'Candy Stripe,' 'Double Crested,' 'Imperial Pink,' 'Sensation Mixed Colors'

**Common name:** Dahlia, Annual
**Scientific name:** *Dahlia* × *hybrida*
**Plant hardiness:** Tender annual. Zones 9–11.

**Optimal growing region and climate:** Dahlias are natives of Mexico and prefer a warm climate.

**Soil temperature for planting:** 60°F (16°C). Sow seeds directly into the garden when all danger of frost has passed. Earlier blooms can be cultivated if you start seeds indoors about 8 weeks before the last frost date.

**Soil needs:** Neutral, 7.0 pH, moist, well-drained soil. Fertility: rich. Feed regularly during the growing season.

**Light preference:** Full sun to partial shade.

**Watering requirement:** Water regularly; avoid allowing the soil to dry out. During bloom, give the plant at least 1 in. (25 mm) of water per week.

**Spacing and size of plants:** 12 in. (30 cm) apart, to 18 in. (45 cm) tall.

**Bloom period/season:** Blooms mid-summer to frost.

**Tips and uses:** Tall dahlias are good in mixed beds and borders. Smaller types can be massed in bed displays. Good cutting flower.

**Cultivars:** 'Figaro Improved,' 'Piccolo,' 'Redskin,' 'Sunny'

**Common name:** Daisy, African

**Scientific name:** *Arctotis stoechadifolia*

**Plant hardiness:** Tender perennial grown as an annual. Zones 2–10.

**Optimal growing region and climate:** A long, cool growing season is best. These plants do well in coastal areas. Ideal temperature is 60–70°F (16–21°C).

**Soil temperature for planting:** 60–70°F (16–21°C). When night temperatures rise to 50°F (10°C) or above, move plants outdoors.

**Soil needs:** Neutral, 7.0 pH, sandy, well-drained soil. Fertility: rich.

**Light preference:** Full sun.

**Watering requirement:** Minimal watering. Allow plants to dry out between waterings.

**Spacing and size of plants:** 6–12 in.(15–30 cm) apart, to 24 in. (60 cm) tall.

**Bloom period/season:** Spring into summer.

**Tips and uses:** Seed deteriorates when stored, so always use fresh seed. Good flower for beds, borders, cut flowers, and containers.

**Cultivars:** 'Mixed Colors,' 'T&M Hybrids'

**Common name:** Daisy, Dahlberg; or Golden Fleece

**Scientific name:** *Dyssodia tenuiloba*

**Plant hardiness:** Tender annual or short-lived perennial. Zones 2–11.

**Optimal growing region and climate:** This is a good flower for southern gardens because it thrives during long spells of hot weather. Native to Texas and Mexico.

**Soil temperature for planting:** 60–80°F (16–27°C). In zones 3–8, sow indoors 10–12 weeks before the last frost; transplant outside after frost danger has passed. For zones 9–11, plant outdoors any time in the autumn or early spring (before or after frost).

**Soil needs:** Neutral, 7.0 pH, well-drained to dry, sandy soil. Fertility: moderate. Avoid overfeeding.

**Light preference:** Full sun.
**Watering requirement:** Water sparingly.
**Spacing and size of plants:** 9–12 in. (30 cm) apart, to 12 in. (30 cm) tall.
**Bloom period/season:** Early summer to frost.
**Tips and uses:** Good for edging beds, borders, or as a ground cover. Resists pests and diseases.
**Cultivars:** Not sold by varietal name.

**Common name:** Daisy, Swan River
**Scientific name:** *Brachycome iberidifolia*
**Plant hardiness:** Half-hardy annual. Zones 2–10.
**Optimal growing region and climate:** Prefers cooler weather. Flowering declines under hot weather conditions. Australian native; common name refers to its native region. Ideal outdoor temperature: 65–70°F (18–21°C).
**Soil temperature for planting:** 60–70°F (16–21°C). Seeds can be sown directly in the garden after all danger of frost has past. Earlier bloom can be forced by starting seeds indoors 6 weeks before the final frost.
**Soil needs:** Neutral, 7.0 pH, well-drained sandy, loose soil. Fertility: rich.
**Light preference:** Full sun to partial shade.
**Watering requirement:** Keep the soil moist.
**Spacing and size of plants:** 6–12 in. (15–30 cm) apart, to 18 in. (45 cm) tall.
**Bloom period/season:** Peak bloom hits in late spring to early summer.
**Tips and uses:** Fragrant flowers can be massed for a lovely effect.
Excellent in hanging baskets and as edging. Pinch tips of young plants encouraging bushiness.
**Cultivars:** 'Bravo,' 'New Amethyst,' 'Splendor,' 'Summer Skies'

**Common name:** Dusty Miller or Cineraria
**Scientific name:** *Senecio* × *hybridus*
**Plant hardiness:** Perennial grown as tender annual. Zones 3–10.
**Optimal growing region and climate:** Likes a cool climate and does best in coastal California, the Pacific Northwest, coastal British Columbia, and high-elevation areas; not frost tolerant. Ideal outdoor temperature: 65–75°F (18–24°C).
**Soil temperature for planting:** 70–80°F (21–27°C). Most easily grown from spring transplants as seeds take several months to flower. In zones 9–10, sow seeds outdoors in autumn or early spring. Plants will reseed naturally in climates that suit them.
**Soil needs:** Neutral, 7.0 pH, moist, loose, and well-drained soil. Fertility: rich. Feed occasionally with a liquid fertilizer.
**Light preference:** Full sun to light shade.
**Watering requirement:** Water frequently; do not allow plants to dry out.
**Spacing and size of plants:** 8–10 in. (20–25 cm) apart, to 12 in. (30 cm) tall.
**Bloom period/season:** Spring to early summer. Late winter to early spring in mild-winter climates.
**Tips and uses:** Works well in containers and as a plant for garden beds.
**Cultivars:** 'Hybrid Grandiflora,' 'Improved Festival,' 'Multiflora Scarlet,' 'Silverdust'

**Common name:** Everlasting or Strawflower
**Scientific name:** *Helipterum roseum*
**Plant hardiness:** Tender annual. Zones 3–10.

**Optimal growing region and climate:** An Australian native. Prefers warm weather but is not heat resistant.

**Soil temperature for planting:** 70–85°F (21–29°C). Not an easy transplant, but where summers are short, start indoors 6–8 weeks before final frost. Transplant outdoors when the soil has warmed above 80°F (27°C). Sow directly outside in late spring after frost danger has passed.

**Soil needs:** Neutral to alkaline, 7.0–7.5 pH, moist, well-drained sandy soil. Fertility: moderately rich. Tolerates poor soils.

**Light preference:** Full sun.

**Watering requirement:** Water only during dry spells.

**Spacing and size of plants:** 6–12 in. (15–30 cm) apart, to 2 ft. (60 cm) tall.

**Bloom period/season:** Summer bloom.

**Tips and uses:** Widely used for cutting and dried arrangements. To dry cut flowers, hang them blossom-end down in a dry, shady place.

**Cultivars:** Usually sold as a mixture. May be sold as 'Accroclinium' or 'Rhodanthe.'

**Common name:** Firecracker Plant
**Scientific name:** *Cuphea ignea*
**Plant hardiness:** Tender annual. Zones 3–11.
**Optimal growing region and climate:** A warm-weather plant native to Mexico. Tolerates heat and humidity well. Best if night temperatures are 50°F (10°C) or higher; ideal daytime range is 68–72°F (20–22°C).
**Soil temperature for planting:** 70–85°F (21–29°C). Start seeds indoors 8–10 weeks before last spring frost. Set out transplants in the garden when the soil warms. Sow directly into garden in zones 9–11.
**Soil needs:** Neutral, 7.0 pH, well-drained, loose soil. Fertility: moderate to rich. Fertilize every 2 weeks.
**Light preference:** Full sun.
**Watering requirement:** Keep soil moist.
**Spacing and size of plants:** 9 in. (22 cm) apart, to 12 in. (30 cm) tall.
**Bloom period/season:** Summer to autumn flowers.
**Tips and uses:** Spider mites can be a problem. Makes a nice color accent for gardens, massed in front of a border, and is attractive in containers.
**Cultivars:** Not sold by varietal name.

**Common name:** Flax, Flowering
**Scientific name:** *Linum grandiflorum*
**Plant hardiness:** Hardy annual. Zones 2–9.
**Optimal growing region and climate:** Prefers cool weather, especially cool summers. Tolerates mild frost. Ideal outdoor temperature: 65–70°F (18–21°C). Native to Algeria.
**Soil temperature for planting:** 60–70°F (16–21°C). Difficult to transplant. Will grow quickly from seeds sown outdoors in early spring. Sow in the autumn in mild climates. Plants will often reseed themselves.
**Soil needs:** Neutral, 7.0 pH, well-drained, sandy loam. Fertility: moderately rich to rich. Ordinary soil is fine.

**Light preference:** Full sun to light shade.

**Watering requirement:** Water lightly, but keep soil moist during dry spells.

**Spacing and size of plants:** 6 in. (15 cm) apart, to 2 ft. (60 cm) tall. Tolerates some crowding.

**Bloom period/season:** Spring into summer. Sow successively during the season to prolong the blooming period. Each plant provides flowers for 3–4 weeks.

**Tips and uses:** Excellent color for mixed beds, and borders. Nice in cottage and meadow gardens.

**Cultivars:** 'Bright Eyes,' 'Diamint White,' 'Rubrum.'

**Common name:** Flossflower

**Scientific name:** *Ageratum houstonianum*

**Plant hardiness:** Tender annual. Zones 4–11.

**Optimal growing region and climate:** Does well in every zone except the coldest. Found in Central and South America as well as the southern U.S. Ideal outdoor temperature: 70–75°F (21–24°C).

**Soil temperature for planting:** 70–85°F (21–29°C). Small seedlings can be swamped by weeds, making it hard to sow directly. Start indoors and set out transplants after all frost danger has passed. In milder zones, plant the seeds in late summer for autumn flowers.

**Soil needs:** Neutral, 7.0 pH, moist, well-drained soil. Fertility: rich. Enrich with manure or compost.

**Light preference:** Full sun, except in very hot weather areas where partial shade should be provided.

**Watering requirement:** Keep the soil moist but not overwatered through the growing season.

**Spacing and size of plants:** 6–9 in. (15–23 cm) apart, to 30 in. (75 cm) tall.

**Bloom period/season:** A long-lasting bloom from early summer to autumn.

**Tips and uses:** Excellent for cutting. Scald the stems after picking and soak in cool water before arranging. Very popular as an edger.

**Cultivars:** 'Album,' 'Blue Blazer,' 'North Sea,' 'Summer Snow'

**Common name:** Forget-Me-Not, Garden

**Scientific name:** *Myosotis sylvatica*

**Plant hardiness:** Hardy annual or biennial. Zones 5-8.

**Optimal growing region and climate:** Cool, moist conditions suit this plant best. Ideal outdoor temperature: 55–65°F (13–18°C). A native of Europe and Asia.

**Soil temperature for planting:** 70°F (21°C). In regions with a short growing season, sow seeds outdoors in early spring. In mild-winter regions, sow in the autumn for spring color. Once established, plants will self-seed.

**Soil needs:** Neutral, 7.0 pH, moist, well-drained soil. Fertility: moderate to rich. Enrich the soil with organic matter.

**Light preference:** Full sun (partial shade if sunlight is intense).

**Watering requirement:** Water during dry periods; keep the soil lightly moist.

**Spacing and size of plants:** 6–8 in. (15–20 cm) apart, to 2 ft. (60 cm) tall.

**Bloom period/season:** The bloom peaks in spring, but continues into summer and autumn. Will bloom in winter in mild areas.

**Tips and uses:** A classic of the English garden. Good as a ground cover, especially with spring bulbs. Also for use in edging, beds, borders, and rock gardens.

**Cultivars:** 'Blue Bird,' 'Carmine King,' 'Ultramarine,' 'Victoria Blue'

**Common name:** Four O'clock or Marvel of Peru

**Scientific name:** *Mirabilis jalapa*

**Plant hardiness:** Commonly grown as a tender annual. Zones 8–11.

**Optimal growing region and climate:** A native of Peru and the American tropics. It is heat, humidity, and air-pollution resistant and frost tender.

**Soil temperature for planting:** 70–85°F (21–29°C). Start seeds indoors 4–6 weeks before the last frost date or sow outdoors after all danger of frost has passed.

**Soil needs:** Neutral, 7.0 pH, well-drained to dry, sandy soil. Fertility: average to rich. Feed monthly and supplement with organic materials such as compost and leaf mold. Tolerates poor soil.

**Light preference:** Full sun to partial shade.

**Watering requirement:** Water regularly.

**Spacing and size of plants:** 1–2 ft. (30–60 cm) apart, to 3 ft. (90 cm) tall.

**Bloom period/season:** Flowers summer to autumn. The sweetly scented flowers open in the afternoon.

**Tips and uses:** These plants can survive the winter if the tubers are dug up in the autumn and stored in a frost-free area. Generally resistant to pests and disease. Use as a low shrub or hedge or in flower beds and borders. Also good around patios and pools.

**Cultivars:** 'Jingles,' 'Teatime'

**Common name:** Geranium, Common

**Scientific name:** *Pelargonium* X *hortorum*

**Plant hardiness:** Tender annual. Zones 4–10.

**Optimal growing region and climate:** This family of flowers, native to South Africa, is America's most popular flowering plant. It is partial to warm weather, but intense heat and humidity will kill it. Ideal outdoor temperature: 70–75°F (21–24°C).

**Soil temperature for planting:** 70–85°F (21–29°C). Set out transplants or cuttings 1 week after last frost. Start seeds indoors 8–10 weeks before the last frost.

**Soil needs:** Neutral, 7.0 pH, well-drained soil. Fertility: moderate to rich. Supplement with lime and feed regularly.

**Light preference:** Full sun.

**Watering requirement:** Water regularly. Let the soil become moderately dry between waterings.

**Spacing and size of plants:** 12–18 in. (30–45 cm) apart, to 3 ft. (90 cm) tall.

**Bloom period/season:** Flowers spring through autumn.

**Tips and uses:** Geraniums grown from seed are less likely to be affected by fungi and viruses than those raised from cuttings. Generally pest free. Traditional in pots, but also a very popular bedding plant. Good in borders, hanging baskets, containers, and as a houseplant.

**Cultivars:** 'Freckles,' 'Hollywood Star,' 'Mrs. Parker,' 'Orange Appeal'

**Common name:** Geranium, Trailing

**Scientific name:** *Pelargonium peltatum*

**Plant hardiness:** Perennial grown as tender annual. Zones 9–10.

**Optimal growing region and climate:** A South African native partial to warm weather, but intense heat and humidity will kill it. Does well in areas with night temperatures of 45–65°F (7–18°C).

**Soil temperature for planting:** 70–75°F (21–24°C). Start seeds indoors 8–10 weeks before last frost. Set out transplants 1 week after the final frost.

**Soil needs:** Neutral, 7.0 pH, moist, well-drained soil. Fertility: moderately rich. Fertilize every 2 weeks from spring through autumn.

**Light preference:** Full sun.

**Watering preference:** Water well and regularly, but let soil dry moderately between waterings.

**Spacing and size of plants:** 12–18 in. (30–45 cm) apart, to 3 ft. (90 cm) long.

**Bloom period/season:** Flowers spring through autumn.

**Tips and uses:** Excellently suited for hanging baskets and windowboxes. If you plant in containers, move the plants to larger pots before they become root bound. Pinch tips back once or twice in the spring to encourage branching.

**Cultivars:** 'Breakaway Hybrid,' 'Summer Showers'

**Common name:** Heliotrope or Cherry Pie

**Scientific name:** *Heliotropium arborescens*

**Plant hardiness:** Perennial treated as annual. Zones 10–11.

**Optimal growing region and climate:** This warm-weather plant does not like cold or exposure and is very frost sensitive. A native of Peru. Night temperatures should be at or above 55°F (13°C) for this plant to thrive.

**Soil temperature for planting:** 70–85°F (21–29°C). Start seeds indoors 6–8 weeks before last frost date. Transplants can be set out when the soil has warmed. Blooms for a long period and can be grown as an evergreen shrub in warm zones.

**Soil needs:** Neutral, 7.0 pH, well-drained soil. Fertility: moderate to rich. Fertilize every 2 weeks.

**Light preference:** Full sun.

**Watering requirement:** Water well, especially during dry spells.

**Spacing and size of plants:** 12 in. (30 cm) apart, to 4 ft. (1.2 m) tall.

**Bloom period/season:** Flowers in summer.

**Tips and uses:** Winters easily as an indoor plant. Remove faded flowers to promote new blooms. Works as a nice accent plant in mixed beds and borders as well as containers. Perfume is distilled from the blossoms.

**Cultivars:** 'Black Beauty,' 'Iowa,' 'Marine,' 'Mini Marine'

**Common name:** Hollyhock

**Scientific name:** *Alcea rosea*

**Plant hardiness:** Hardy biennial with an annual strain. Zones 3–9.

**Optimal growing region and climate:** This native of China is partial to warm climates.

**Soil temperature for planting:** 70–85°F (21–29°C). Seeds can be started indoors 6–8 weeks before last frost date. Set plants outside as the weather warms.

**Soil needs:** Neutral, 7.0 pH, moist, loamy, well-drained soil. Fertility: average to rich. Benefits from regular applications of liquid fertilizer during the growing season.

**Light preference:** Full sun.

**Watering requirement:** Water heavily during the growing season, then reduce after flowering.

**Spacing and size of plants:** 18–24 in. (45–60 cm) apart, to 10 ft. (3 m) tall.

**Bloom period/season:** Summer to early autumn.

**Tips and uses:** Dust rust-infected plants with sulfur, and control mites with insecticidal soap spray. Stake if the site is windy. This stately plant makes a nice background highlight in borders and can be used as a screen. Its foliage is particularly good for gates and doorways. For autumn bloom, cut stems to the ground from mature plantings and feed with a good garden fertilizer.

**Cultivars:** 'Chater's Giants,' 'Majorette,' 'Powder Puff,' 'Summer Carnival'

**Common name:** Impatiens or Busy Lizzie

**Scientific name:** *Impatiens wallerana*

**Plant hardiness:** Perennial grown as tender annual. Zones 2–10.

**Optimal growing region and climate:** Does particularly well in temperatures of 70–75°F (21–24°C) and loves humidity. Garden varieties developed from plants native to India and Africa.

**Soil temperature for planting:** 70–80°F (21–27°C). Transplant or sow seed after all danger of frost has passed.

**Soil needs:** Neutral, 7.0 pH, well-drained, moist and sandy soil. Fertility: rich. Feed monthly with all-purpose fertilizer.

**Light preference:** Part shade to full shade.

**Watering requirement:** Water and mist plants often, but let the soil dry out between waterings.

**Spacing and size of plants:** 10–12 in. (25–30 cm) apart, to 3 ft. (90 cm) tall.

**Bloom period/season:** Blooms early summer to autumn. Blooms best when weather is warm.

**Tips and uses:** Perfect for the shady garden. Excellent accent plants to ring trees and as ground cover. Pinch back to encourage bushiness.

**Cultivars:** 'Mega,' 'Shady Lady,' 'Showstopper Pink and White,' 'Super Elfin'

**Common name:** Johnny-Jump-up

**Scientific name:** *Viola tricolor*

**Plant hardiness:** Hardy annual or short-lived perennial. Zones 3–11.

**Optimal growing region and climate:** Prefers cool weather but is heat resistant. Ideal outdoor temperature: 65–75°F (18–24°C). A native of Europe; has become naturalized in North America.

**Soil temperature for planting:** 70°F (21°C). Start seeds 10–12 weeks before the last spring frost to produce a late spring bloom. In zones 9–11, grow outdoors all winter. Often reseeds itself.

**Soil needs:** Neutral, 7.0 pH, moist, well-drained soil. Fertility: moderately rich. Will grow in almost any soil and location. Regular feedings are fine.

**Light preference:** Full sun to light shade.

**Watering requirement:** Keep the soil moist but not soggy.

**Spacing and size of plants:** 4–6 in. (10–15 cm) apart, to 8 in. (20 cm) tall.

**Bloom period/season:** Blooms early spring to early summer; late winter to spring in mild-winter climates.

**Tips and uses:** Excellent for planting over tulip and daffodil beds. Also makes a nice border for vegetable beds. Useful for edging, rock gardens, and containers. Has been used as a medicinal herb to treat skin problems and as a therapeutic tea.

**Cultivar:** Johnny-Jump-up is variety name.

**Common name:** Kale, Ornamental; or Ornamental Cabbage

**Scientific name:** *Brassica oleracea*

**Plant hardiness:** Hardy annual to perennial; sometimes biennial. Zones 2–10.

**Optimal growing region and climate:** Prefers cool weather. Ideal outdoor temperature: 65–70°F (18–21°C). A frost-resistant plant native to northwest Europe.

**Soil temperature for planting:** 65–85°F (18–29°C). For spring growth, start indoors 8–10 weeks before frost danger has passed. Set into the garden as soon as the soil can be worked. In areas with a cool autumn climate, start in late summer to mature before frost is expected. Leaf colors are richer in cooler weather.

**Soil needs:** Neutral, 7.0 pH, moist, loose, well-drained soil. Fertility: moderately rich.

**Light preference:** Full sun.

**Watering requirement:** Keep the soil moist, especially during dry spells.

**Spacing and size of plants:** 12–24 in. (30–60 cm) apart, to 20 in. (50 cm) tall.

**Bloom period/season:** Foliage is striking throughout spring and autumn, and even into winter in mild climates.

**Tips and uses:** Like all members of the mustard family, ornamental kale is attractive to larvae and caterpillars. Use organic or synthetic control sprays. Excellent for pattern plantings and does well in large containers and windowboxes.

**Cultivar:** 'Dynasty Pink.' Mostly offered in hybrid colors.

**Common name:** Larkspur, Rocket, or Annual Delphinium

**Scientific name:** *Consolida ambigua*

**Plant hardiness:** Hardy annual. Zones 4–8.

**Optimal growing region and climate:** Does very well in cool coastal valleys of California, the Pacific Northwest, and coastal British Columbia. A native of southern Europe. Temperatures of 40–50°F (4–10°C) are ideal for this plant.

**Soil temperature for planting:** 70–85°F (21–29°C). Difficult to transplant; sow seed in very early spring or in autumn.

**Soil needs:** Alkaline, 7.5 pH, moist, well-drained soil. Fertility: rich. Supplement with organic matter and feed occasionally.

**Light preference:** Full sun.

**Watering requirement:** Keep the soil moist.

**Spacing and size of plants:** 16–18 in. (40–45 cm) apart, to 4 ft. (1.2 m) tall.

**Bloom period/season:** Spring and early summer in warmer zones; mid- to late summer and early autumn in cooler ones. Flowers best in cooler areas.

**Tips and uses:** Cut from the garden when lowest flowers are fully open and the top buds show color. A good cutting flower that also is useful for drying. Nice in meadow and cottage gardens and borders.

**Cultivars:** 'Blue Fountains,' 'Blue Heaven,' 'Dwarf Blue Butterfly,' 'Pacific Giants'

**Common name:** Lobelia

**Scientific name:** *Lobelia erinus*

**Plant hardiness:** Half-hardy annual or perennial. Zones 3–9.

**Optimal growing region and climate:** A cool, dry climate is preferable, especially in the summer. Ideal outdoor temperature: 65–75°F (18–24°C). A South African native.

**Soil temperature for planting:** 70–85°F (21–29°C). In the spring, these are easy to grow from nursery transplants, but if you start from seed, sow indoors 10–12 weeks before the final frost. In either case, plant outside 2–3 weeks after the final frost.

**Soil needs:** Neutral, 7.0 pH, sandy, moist, well-drained soil. Fertility: rich. Add humus.

**Light preference:** Full to sun to partial shade in hot-summer areas.

**Watering requirement:** Water frequently, especially during hot weather.

**Spacing and size of plants:** 4–6 in. (10–15 cm) apart, to 8 in. (20 cm) tall.

**Bloom period/season:** Spring to autumn frost.

**Tips and uses:** To encourage growth, pinch off tops when seedlings are 1 in. (25 mm) high. A good bedding and edging plant. Also works very well in rock gardens and rock wall niches.

**Cultivars:** 'Compact Royal Jewels,' 'Crystal Palace,' 'Heavenly,' 'Rosamund'

**Common name:** Love-in-a-Mist

**Scientific name:** *Nigella damascena*

**Plant hardiness:** Hardy annual. Zones 2–10.

**Optimal growing region and climate:** This southern European native prefers cooler growing seasons. Temperatures 70–80°F (21–27°C) encourage continual flowering and large blooms.

**Soil temperature for planting:** 60°F (16°C). Avoid transplanting; sow seeds in the garden as soon as soil can be worked.

**Soil needs:** Neutral, 7.0 pH, dry or gravelly well-drained soil. Fertility: moderately rich. Fertilize monthly.

**Light preference:** Full sun.

**Watering requirement:** Water only when the soil is dry.

**Spacing and size of plants:** 12 in. (30 cm) apart, to 18 in. (45 cm).

**Bloom period/season:** Spring through summer. Repeated sowings will extend the bloom, as will cool temperatures.

**Tips and uses:** Nice in a cottage garden. After the flowers fade, seed pods are puffed up and attractive for dried flower arrangements. In fresh arrangements, the foliage of the plant lends its beautiful, fine texture to the mix. Deadhead to prolong flowering.

**Cultivars:** 'Dwarf Moody Blue,' 'Miss Jekyll,' 'Persian Jewels,' 'Transformer'

**Common name:** Love-Lies-Bleeding or Tassel Flower

**Scientific name:** *Amaranthus caudatus*

**Plant hardiness:** Half-hardy annual. Zones 2–10.

**Optimal growing region and climate:** A heat- and drought-tolerant plant native to India. Ideal temperature: 70–75°F (21–24°C).

**Soil temperature for planting:** 70–85°F (21–29°C). Avoid transplanting; sow seeds when night temperatures reach 50°F (10°C) or higher.

**Soil needs:** Neutral to alkaline, 7.0–7.5 pH, well-drained to dry soil. Fertility: rich.

**Light preference:** Full sun.

**Watering requirement:** Water lightly.

**Spacing and size of plants:** 2 ft. (60 cm) apart, to 4 ft. (120 cm) or taller.

**Bloom period/season:** Blooms summer to first frost.

**Tips and uses:** Good background or accent plant. Makes a dramatic addition to walls and fences. Flowers can be air dried for winter bouquets.

**Cultivars:** 'Green Thumb,' 'Pygmy Torch'

**Common name:** Mallow Wort

**Scientific name:** *Malope trifida*

**Plant hardiness:** Hardy annual. Zones 3–9.

**Optimal growing region and climate:** Not heat resistant; works best in areas where summers are cool. A native of Europe and North Africa.

**Soil temperature for planting:** 65–75°F (18–24°C). Sow seeds indoors 4–6 weeks before the last frost. Transplant seedlings into garden when all danger of frost has passed or sow seed directly into the garden as soon as the soil can be worked, usually a couple of weeks before the final frost.

**Soil needs:** Neutral, 7.0 pH, well-drained, light, sandy loam. Fertility: average to moderately rich. An overly fertile soil will produce dense foliage at the expense of flowers.

**Light preference:** Full sun.

**Watering requirement:** Water moderately.

**Spacing and size of plants:** 9–12 in. (22–30 cm) apart, to 2–3 ft. (60–90 cm) tall.

**Bloom period/season:** Summer.

**Tips and uses:** Good in flower beds and for cutting.

**Cultivars:** 'Alba,' 'Grandiflora,' 'Pink Queen,' 'Rosea,' 'Vulcan,' 'White Queen'

**Common name:** Marigold

**Scientific name:** *Tagetes erecta*

**Plant hardiness:** Half-hardy annual. Zones 3–10.

**Optimal growing region and climate:** Grows in all but the coldest climates. Prefers warm weather, but easy to grow under most conditions. Ideal outdoor temperature: 70–75°F (21–24°C). A native of Argentina and Northern Mexico.

**Soil temperature for planting:** 70–85°F (21–29°C). Start seeds indoors 6–8 weeks before the last frost, or sow seeds outdoors 2–3 weeks after the last frost. One of the easiest garden plants to grow.

**Soil needs:** Neutral, 7.0 pH, moist, well-drained soil. Fertility: average. Fertilize once a month. Tolerates a range of soils.

**Light preference:** Full sun.

**Watering requirement:** Water regularly and deeply, especially when weather is hot and soil is dry.

**Spacing and size of plants:** 8–16 in. (20–40 cm) apart, to 3 ft. (90 cm) tall.

**Bloom period/season:** Early summer until frost. A long-blooming plant.

**Tips and uses:** Marigolds are often planted with other flowers because of their reputation for repelling garden pests. Remove dead blossoms to encourage blooms. Useful for bedding and edging, in borders and containers, and as a kitchen herb.

**Cultivars:** 'French Vanilla,' 'Gem Series,' 'Orange Hawaii,' 'Petite'

**Common name:** Marigold, Cape
**Scientific name:** *Dimorphotheca pluvialis*
**Plant hardiness:** Tender annual. Zones 2–10.
**Optimal growing region and climate:** These plants prefer a cool growing season, including cool summers. Ideal temperature: 60–70°F (16–21°C). Excellent in coastal gardens after threat of frost is over.
**Soil temperature for planting:** 60–70°F (16–21°C). Flowers best when night temperatures are 45–50°F (7–10°C).
**Soil needs:** Neutral, 7.0 pH, well-drained soil. Fertility: average. Feed sparingly; do not overfertilize.
**Light preference:** Full sun.
**Watering requirement:** Water sparingly.
**Spacing and size of plants:** 12 in. (30 cm) apart, to 12 in (30 cm) tall.
**Bloom period/season:** Flowers in winter and early spring in mild-winter areas, summer in most other climates.
**Tips and uses:** Deadhead faded flowers to prolong blooming. Good for beds, borders, containers. Not great cutting flowers because they close at night.
**Cultivars:** 'Aurantica Hybrid,' 'Glistening White,' 'Salmon Queen'

**Common name:** Marigold, Pot
**Scientific name:** *Calendula officinalis*
**Plant hardiness:** Hardy annual. Zones 2–10.
**Optimal growing region and climate:** Blooms best under cool summer conditions. Ideal outdoor temperature: 65–70°F (18–21°C). Native to southern Europe.
**Soil temperature for planting:** 70°F (21°C). Sow directly into garden soil in early spring. Sart seeds indoors 6–8 weeks before the last frost. A late-summer planting in warmer zones will provide autumn and winter blooms.
**Soil needs:** Neutral, 7.0 pH, moist, loamy, well-drained soil. Fertility: average to rich. Tolerates lean soil.
**Light preference:** Full sun.
**Watering requirement:** Water regularly.
**Spacing and size of plants:** 6–12 in. (15–30 cm) apart, to 2 ft. (60 cm) tall.
**Bloom period/season:** Spring through autumn; blooms are aided by cooler temperatures.
**Tips and uses:** Traditional as a healing and culinary herb. Good cutting flower and excellent for beds and borders. Leaves have a spicy fragrance. Deadhead to prolong flowering.
**Cultivars:** 'Fiesta,' 'Gypsy Festival,' 'Pacific Apricot,' 'Touch of Red'

**Common name:** Mignonette, Common
**Scientific name:** *Reseda odorata*
**Plant hardiness:** Hardy annual. Zones 2–11.
**Optimal growing region and climate:** Grows best in cool weather. Ideal outdoor temperature: 55–65°F (13–18°C). Native to the Mediterranean, North Africa, and Egypt.
**Soil temperature for planting:** 70–85°F (21–29°C). Avoid transplanting; sow directly into the garden after frost danger has passed. In frost-free areas, sow in late autumn or early winter.

**Soil needs:** Neutral, 7.0 pH, moist, well-drained soil. Fertility: moderately rich.

**Light preference:** Full sun to partial shade.

**Watering requirement:** Keep the soil moist.

**Spacing and size of plants:** 6–12 in. (15–30 cm) apart, to 18 in. (45 cm) tall.

**Bloom period/season:** Spring. A summer sowing will prolong the bloom.

**Tips and uses:** A fast-growing, sweet-scented flower that can be massed for fragrant effect in the garden. Good for a border and makes a nice cut flower, adding perfume to an indoor arrangement. Generally resistant to pests and diseases.

**Cultivars:** 'Grandiflora,' 'Machet,' 'Red Monarch.'

**Common name:** Monkey Flower

**Scientific name:** *Mimulus hybridus*

**Plant hardiness:** Half-hardy annual. Zones 3–10.

**Optimal growing region and climate:** A favorite of the Pacific Northwest and Vancouver, where it thrives under cool, moist, and shady conditions. Does very well in coastal California under similar conditions. A good planting near water. Ideal outdoor temperature: 70–75°F (21–24°C).

**Soil temperature for planting:** 60°F (16°C). Start seeds indoors 10 weeks before the last frost. Can be sown outdoors in late winter in cool and moist weather. Plant in a sheltered and protected spot.

**Soil needs:** Neutral, 7.0 pH, moist, well-drained soil. Fertility: moderately rich. Add organic matter.

**Light preference:** Partial shade to full shade.

**Watering requirement:** Water regularly and keep the soil moist.

**Spacing and size of plants:** 6 in. (15 cm) apart, to 2 ft. (60 cm) tall.

**Bloom period/season:** Summer to autumn. Flowers continuously in cool weather but will stop blooming in heat.

**Tips and uses:** Remove faded blooms to promote further flowering. A great shade garden plant. Useful for bedding, borders, stream, or poolside gardens. Also attractive in rock gardens and rock wall niches. Spreads well for container and hanging basket use.

**Cultivars:** 'Calypso,' 'Malibu Orange,' 'Velvet,' 'Viva'

**Common name:** Morning Glory, Dwarf

**Scientific name:** *Convolvulus tricolor*

**Plant hardiness:** Tender annual. Zones 2–10.

**Optimal growing region and climate:** This plant performs best under dry, sunny conditions and warm weather. A native of southern Europe. Ideal outdoor temperature: 70–80°F (21–27°C).

**Soil temperature for planting:** 70–85°F (21–29°C). Sow seeds after all frost danger has passed and night temperatures remain above 50°F (10°C). In areas with short summers, start seeds indoors 6 weeks before the expected date of the last frost.

**Soil needs:** Acid to neutral to alkaline, 6.5–7.5 pH, well-drained, sandy soil. Fertility: poor to moderately rich. Tolerates poor soil.

**Light preference:** Full sun.

**Watering requirement:** Moderate watering.

**Spacing and size of plants:** 12 in. (30 cm) apart, to 12 in. (30 cm) tall.

**Bloom period/season:** Spring into summer.

**Tips and uses:** To speed germination when planting seeds, nick the hard seed coat with a file. Good in hanging baskets, containers, and windowboxes. Also makes a great edging plant.

**Cultivars:** 'Blue Flash,' 'Blue Ensign,' 'Dwarf Rainbow Flash,' 'Royal Ensign'

**Common name:** Moss Rose

**Scientific name:** *Portulaca grandiflora*

**Plant hardiness:** Tender annual. Zones 9–11.

**Optimal growing region and climate:** Flourishes in sunny, hot, and dry areas, but does well in humidity too. A native of Brazil. Ideal outdoor temperature: 70–85°F (21–29°C).

**Soil temperature for planting:** 70–85°F (21–29°C). Start seeds indoors 4–6 weeks ahead of usual springtime planting dates, or seed outdoors directly after the final frost. Self sows.

**Soil needs:** Neutral, 7.0 pH, dry, sandy, well-drained soil. Loose loam is fine. Fertility: poor to average. Fertilizing is unnecessary and can be harmful.

**Light preference:** Full sun.

**Watering requirement:** Water sparingly.

**Spacing and size of plants:** 6–8 in. (15–20 cm) apart, to 12 in. (30 cm) tall.

**Bloom period/season:** Early summer to late autumn or frost. Flowers open in the sun and close at night.

**Tips and uses:** Works well for sunny slopes, dry banks, as an edging for walls and between stones. Grows nicely in massed beds, rock gardens, and in containers. Prone to aphid attacks.

**Cultivars:** 'Afternoon Delight,' 'Cloudbeater Mix,' 'Sundial,' 'Swan'

**Common name:** Nasturtium, Garden

**Scientific name:** *Tropaeolum majus*

**Plant hardiness:** Tender annual. Zones 3–10.

**Optimal growing region and climate:** Cool, dry conditions are best. Will grow in all but the coldest temperatures but is not a great choice for the southeastern U.S. in the summer. Good growing regions include the northern Pacific and Atlantic coasts of the U.S. and Canada. Native to cool regions of South America.

**Soil temperature for planting:** 65°F (18°C). Hard to transplant but easy to grow from seeds or cuttings planted directly into the garden. Plant outdoors after the final frost. The seeds are large and easy to handle, making it a nice selection for a child's garden.

**Soil needs:** Neutral, 7.0 pH, light, sandy, well-drained soil. Fertility: moderately rich to poor. Do not give supplementary feedings to avoid more foliage than flowers.

**Light preference:** Full sun.

**Watering requirement:** Water every 7–10 days once established.

**Spacing and size of plants:** 8–12 in. (20–30 cm) apart; dwarf varieties to 15 in. (38 cm) tall, climbers to 10 ft. (3 m) long.

**Bloom period/season:** Summer to autumn. Winter to spring in warm-weather climates.

**Tips and uses:** Leaves are edible and have a peppery flavor. Frequent cutting prolongs flowering. Excellent cover for trellises, posts, and rocks. Attractive in hanging baskets and windowboxes.

**Cultivars:** 'Alaska,' 'Double Dwarf Jewel,' 'Empress of India,' 'Whirlybird'

**Common name:** Nemesia, Pouch; or Bluebird
**Scientific name:** *Nemesia strumosa*
**Plant hardiness:** Tender annual. Zones 3–10.
**Optimal growing region and climate:** Nemesia does not like heat and humidity. It is much happier in a temperature range of 55–70°F (13–21°C). A long, cool growing season is best. Well-suited to coastal California, the Pacific Northwest, and British Columbia.
**Soil temperature for planting:** 60°F (16°C). Sow outdoors in cooler climes after frost danger has passed. In warmer areas, start seeds indoors 8–10 weeks before the last frost. In mild-winter areas, sheltered nemesia can bloom into the winter.
**Soil needs:** Acid to neutral, 6.5–7.0 pH, moist, well-drained soil. Fertility: moderately rich. Feed liberally.
**Light preference:** Full sun.
**Watering requirement:** Water regularly, especially during dry periods.
**Spacing and size of plants:** 6 in. (15 cm) apart, to 2 ft. (60 cm) tall.
**Bloom period/season:** Summer. Winter to spring in mild-winter climates.
**Tips and uses:** Pinch tips of seedlings to encourage bushiness. Good for bedding, borders, rock gardens, and rock wall niches. Works in containers and as a cut flower.
**Cultivars:** 'Blue Gem,' 'Carnival Mixed Colors,' 'Mello Red and White,' 'National Ensign'

**Common name:** Painted Tongue or Velvet Flower
**Scientific name:** *Salpiglossis sinuata*
**Plant hardiness:** Half-hardy annual. Zones 2–10.
**Optimal growing region and climate:** Prefers cool weather with little humidity. Grown in winter as a cool greenhouse plant. Ideal outdoor temperature: 70–75°F (21–24°C). Native to South America.
**Soil temperature for planting:** 70–85°F (21–29°C). Start seeds indoors in the early spring. Transplant to the garden 2 weeks before the last frost. Larger transplants makes for hardier, longer-blooming plants.
**Soil needs:** Neutral, 7.0 pH, moist, well-drained soil. Fertility: rich. Supplement with organic matter, but avoid overfeeding plants; they are sensitive to nitrogen burn.
**Light preference:** Full sun.
**Watering requirement:** Water lightly.
**Spacing and size of plants:** 8–12 in. (20–30 cm) apart, to 30 in. (75 cm) tall.
**Bloom period/season:** Late spring to early summer. Blooms through the summer only in very cool gardens.
**Tips and uses:** This plant has weak stems, so place it next to sturdier specimens. Nice in borders; adds color and depth to cut-flower bouquets.
**Cultivars:** 'Bolero,' 'Casino,' 'Kew Blue,' 'Royale'

**Common name:** Pansy
**Scientific name:** *Viola cornuta*
**Plant hardiness:** Hardy annual. Zones 3–9.
**Optimal growing region and climate:** Flowers best in cooler weather. Ideal temperature: 65–75°F (18–24°C). Native to northern Spain.

**Soil temperature for planting:** 70°F (21°C). Start seeds indoors 10–12 weeks before the last spring frost for a late spring bloom.

**Soil needs:** Neutral, 7.0 pH, loamy, moist, well-drained soil. Fertility: moderately rich. Apply liquid plant food biweekly.

**Light preference:** Full sun. Provide afternoon shade in warmer areas to prolong the plant's blooms.

**Watering requirement:** Water regularly with a good soaking.

**Spacing and size of plants:** 4–6 in. (10–15 cm) apart, to 12 in. (30 cm) tall.

**Bloom period/season:** Early spring to early summer. Late winter and spring in mild-winter climates.

**Tips and uses:** Useful for bedding and edging, in rock gardens and containers, and as cut flowers. Very nice in beddings with spring bulbs.

**Cultivars:** 'Bluebird,' 'Bowles Back,' 'Sorbet,' 'Yesterday, Today and Tomorrow'

**Common name:** Pepper, Ornamental; or Christmas Pepper

**Scientific name:** *Capsicum annuum*

**Plant hardiness:** Perennial treated as annual. Zones 9–11.

**Optimal growing region and climate:** Warm-weather plants native to tropical Americas.

**Soil temperature for planting:** 75–80°F (24–27°C). Warmth should be consistent when plants are set out in late spring, with night temperatures above 55°F (13°C). In areas that are frost free, sow outdoors in the autumn.

**Soil needs:** Acid to neutral, 6.5–7 pH, moist, loamy, well-drained soil. Fertility: rich. Fertilize twice—first, when plants reach 8 in. (20 cm) high, then again at 12 in. (30 cm).

**Light preference:** Full sun.

**Watering requirement:** Water regularly; keep soil moist.

**Spacing and size of plants:** 6–12 in.(15–30 cm) apart, to 12 in. (30 cm) tall.

**Bloom period/season:** Late summer through autumn. Small flowers are followed by fruit.

**Tips and uses:** Wear gloves to handle peppers to avoiding eye-irritation hazard. Works well in borders and as a container plant. Bring indoors for use as an ornamental holiday plant.

**Cultivars:** 'Fiesta,' 'Holiday Cheer,' 'Red Missile,' 'Treasure Red'

> **Warning**
>
> Always wear gloves whenever handling peppers to avoid eye and skin irritation from the capsaicin they contain.

**Common name:** Petunia

**Scientific name:** *Petunia* x *hybrida*

**Plant hardiness:** Half-hardy annual. Zones 3–10.

**Optimal growing region and climate:** Temperate plant that will tolerate a mild frost. Ideal outdoor temperature: 70–80°F (21–27°C). Native to Argentina; seeds brought to Europe in the 1850s.

**Soil temperature for planting:** Start seeds indoors 10–12 weeks before the last frost. Plant outside after frost danger has passed, though seedlings will survive a mild chill. Shelter from wind and hard rain.

**Soil needs:** Neutral, 7.0 pH, well-drained, sandy loam. Fertility: moderately rich. Supplement with organic matter. Tolerates a variety of soil. Feed once or twice during the growing season to avoid an abundance of foliage at the sacrifice of blooms.

**Light preference:** Full sun to partial shade.

**Watering requirement:** Water regularly to establish, then whenever the soil dries out.

**Spacing and size of plants:** 7–10 in. (18–25 cm) apart, to 12 in. (30 cm) tall.

**Bloom period/season:** A long blooming season from late spring to autumn.

**Tips and uses:** Works well with a variety of flowers; used for bedding, borders, hanging baskets, containers, windowboxes, and as a ground cover. Generally pest and disease free.

**Cultivars:** 'Crimson Star,' 'Glacier,' 'Wave,' 'White Cascade'

**Common name:** Phlox

**Scientific name:** *Phlox drummondii*

**Plant hardiness:** Half-hardy annual. Zones 3–9.

**Optimal growing region and climate:** Heat resistant in dry weather, but does equally well in cooler temperatures of 55–65°F (13–18°C). A native of Texas.

**Soil temperature for planting:** 55–65°F (13–18°C). Sow outdoors in the very early spring. In mild climates, continue planting late summer through autumn. In colder areas with short growing seasons, start seeds indoors 8–10 weeks before last frost; place outside 2–3 weeks before final frost has passed.

**Soil needs:** Acidic to neutral, 6.5–7.0 pH, moist to dry well-drained soil. Fertility: average to moderately rich. Feed monthly.

**Light preference:** Full sun to partial shade.

**Watering requirement:** Water well, keep soil evenly moist, especially through hot, dry weather.

**Spacing and size of plants:** 10–12 in. (25–30 cm) apart, to 20 in. (50 cm) tall. Phlox requires ample spacing and good air circulation to avoid problems with powdery mildew.

**Bloom period/season:** Long flowering from summer to autumn.

**Tips and uses:** Shear plant back to promote new growth. Used for bedding, edging, containers, rock gardens and cottage gardens. A good ground cover around summer blooming bulbs.

**Cultivars:** 'Dwarf Beauty,' 'Glamour,' 'Phlox of Sheep,' 'Twinkle Mixed'

**Common name:** Pincushion Flower or Sweet Scabious

**Scientific name:** *Scabiosa atropurpurea*

**Plant hardiness:** Half-hardy annual. Zones 4–10.

**Optimal growing region and climate:** Flowers best in climates with mild summer temperatures. Will tolerate mild frost. A native of southern Europe that has naturalized in California.

**Soil temperature for planting:** 70°F (21°C). Sow seeds directly into the garden in early spring after the soil has warmed. Sowing also can take place in the autumn in mild-winter climates.

**Soil needs:** Neutral to alkaline, 7.0–7.5 pH, loose, well-drained soil. Avoid acidic soils. Fertility: average to moderately rich.

**Light preference:** Full sun.

**Watering requirement:** Water moderately during dry spells.

**Spacing and size of plants:** 12 in. (30 cm) apart, to 24 in. (60 cm) tall.

**Bloom period/season:** Summer to autumn.

**Tips and uses:** One of the best cut flowers for a fresh flower arrangement, it's also effective in a dried flower arrangement. Flowerheads dry right on the plant and can be collected from the garden. Scabiosa is derived from the word scabies, meaning itch, and supposedly has properties that cure skin irritations. Works nicely as a background highlight in mixed beds and in borders.

**Cultivars:** 'Butterfly Blue,' 'Giant Imperial,' 'Paper Moon,' 'Ping Pong'

**Common name:** Poppy, California
**Scientific name:** *Eschscholzia californica*
**Plant hardiness:** Hardy annual or perennial. Zones 8–10.
**Optimal growing region and climate:** California's state flower. Prefers cool nights. Drought tolerant. Ideal outdoor temperature: 60–65°F (16–18°C).
**Soil temperature for planting:** 60°F (16°C). Easy to grow by planting seed outdoors in early spring as soon as the soil can be worked for blooms in early summer. In mild-winter climates, seeds sown in the autumn will grow and bear early spring flowers.
**Soil needs:** Neutral to alkaline, 7.0–7.5 pH, dry, sandy, well-drained soil. Fertility: moderately rich.
**Light preference:** Full sun.
**Watering requirement:** Water sparingly; do not overwater.
**Spacing and size of plants:** 6–8 in. (15–20 cm) apart, to 24-in. (60 cm) tall.
**Bloom period/season:** Flowers spring through early summer during cool weather.
**Tips and uses:** Self sows in warm climates. Great in beds, borders, and rock gardens. Very nice wildflower mix.
**Cultivars:** 'Alba,' 'Aurantiaca,' 'Ballerina Series,' 'Compacta,' 'Crocea,' 'Dalli,' 'Monarch Art Shades,' 'Rosea,' 'Thai Silk'

**Common name:** Poppy, Flanders; or Shirley Poppy
**Scientific name:** *Papaver rhoeas*
**Plant hardiness:** Hardy annual. Zones 5–10.
**Optimal growing region and climate:** Performs best under cool conditions. Good for winter and early spring color in the desert Southwest and deep South. Ideal outdoor temperature: 70–75°F (21–24°C).
**Soil temperature for planting:** 60–70°F (16–21°C). Not good transplants. Sow seeds directly into the garden several weeks before the last frost date; seedlings will tolerate mild frosts. Sow successions 4–6 weeks apart to keep the bloom going.
**Soil needs:** Acid to neutral, 6.5–7.0 pH, well-drained, sandy soil. Fertility: average to rich.
**Light preference:** Full sun.
**Watering requirement:** Keep the soil lightly moist.
**Spacing and size of plants:** 12 in. (30 cm) apart, to 3 ft. (90 cm) tall.
**Bloom period/season:** Blooms spring through early summer. Plants bloom best when nights are cool; hot weather will cut the flowering period short.
**Tips and uses:** Good choice for wildflower gardens; will self sow. Pick off dead flowers to encourage blooms. The dried seeds can be used as a topping for baked goods.
**Cultivars:** 'Double-Flowered,' 'Legion of Honor,' 'Mother of Pearl,' 'Single-Flowered'

**Common name:** Poppy, Iceland
**Scientific name:** *Papaver nudicaule*
**Plant hardiness:** Half-hardy annual. Zones 5–10.

**Optimal growing region and climate:** Performs best under cool conditions. A native of Canada and the Pacific Northwest. Good for winter and early spring color in mild-winter climates. Ideal outdoor temperature: 70–75°F (21–24°C).

**Soil temperature for planting:** 60–70°F (16–21°C). Avoid transplanting. Sow seeds outdoors in early spring as soon as the ground can be worked (even before the last frost date).

**Soil needs:** Neutral, 7.0 pH, well-drained, loam. Fertility: moderately rich.

**Light preference:** Full sun. Will tolerate light shade.

**Watering requirement:** Keep the soil a little moist.

**Spacing and size of plants:** 12 in. (30 cm) apart, to 24 in. (60 cm) tall.

**Bloom period/season:** Spring through early summer. Blooms best during cool, sunny weather.

**Tips and uses:** Excellent as a cut flower. Cut while the flowers are still buds and sear the stems in boiling water or over a flame. Picking off dead flowers increases the bloom.

**Cultivars:** 'Champagne Bubbles,' 'Oregon Rainbows,' 'Red Sails,' 'Wonderland Mixed'

> **Warning**
>
> Foliage and seeds of Iceland poppies are hazardous if ingested. Avoid planting in areas frequented by pets or children.

---

**Common name:** Primrose
**Scientific name:** *Primula malacoides*
**Plant hardiness:** Short-lived perennials treated as annuals. Zones 5–8.
**Optimal growing climate and region:** Prefers cool weather and moist conditions. Cannot tolerate heat. Woodlands and streamside settings are perfect. Excellent plant for Pacific Northwest, coastal British Columbia. A European native.
**Soil temperature for planting:** 60–70°F (16–21°C). Nursery-grown transplants are best as they are difficult to grow from seed. Set out in spring; in mild-winter areas, set out in early autumn.
**Soil needs:** Acid to neutral, 6.5–7.0 pH, moist, loose, well-drained soil. Fertility: rich. Add high organic matter with peat moss and compost.
**Light preference:** Partial shade.
**Watering requirement:** Water regularly. Avoid allowing the soil to dry out.
**Spacing and size of plants:** 6 in. (15 cm) apart, to 4–18 in. (10–45 cm) tall.
**Bloom period/season:** Spring. Will bloom mid-winter in mild-climate areas.
**Tips and uses:** The fragrant flowers attract bees and butterflies. Use as a mass planting in beds and borders, especially in partially shaded areas.
**Cultivars:** 'Cantata,' 'First Love,' 'Pacific Giants,' 'Rosea'

---

**Common name:** Rose-of-Heaven or Campion
**Scientific name:** *Lychnis coeli-rosa*
**Plant hardiness:** Half-hardy annual. Zones 2–10.
**Optimal growing region and climate:** Prefers warm weather, but also grows wild in northern temperate zones as well as sections of the Arctic. Native to Russia.
**Soil temperature for planting:** 70°F (21°C). Sow directly into the garden in early spring; tolerates mild frost. Place transplants in the garden in spring, when tulip bulbs start to bloom.
**Soil needs:** Neutral, 7.0 pH, dry, well-drained soil. Fertility: moderately rich to rich.

**Light preference:** Full sun.
**Watering requirement:** Water sparingly; prefers drier soil conditions.
**Spacing and size of plants:** 4 in. (10 cm) apart, to 8–20 in. (20–50 cm) tall.
**Bloom period/season:** Summer; winter to spring in mild-winter climates.
**Tips and uses:** An excellent container flower. Good for beds and cutting.
**Cultivars:** 'Candida,' 'Kermesina,' 'Nana,' 'Nobilis'

**Common name:** Safflower or False Saffron
**Scientific name:** *Carthamus tinctorius*
**Plant hardiness:** Hardy annual. Zones 2–10.
**Optimal growing region and climate:** Does best in dry climates; fares poorly in rainy, humid areas. A native of Egypt.
**Soil temperature for planting:** 55–65°F (13–18°C). Sow seeds outdoors after all danger of frost has passed.
**Soil needs:** Neutral to alkaline, 7.0–7.5 pH, light, dry soil. Fertility: poor. Grows easily under average to poor conditions.
**Light preference:** Full sun.
**Watering requirement:** Water sparingly.
**Spacing and size of plants:** 4–6 in. (15 cm) apart, to 3 ft. (90 cm) tall.
**Bloom period/season:** Flowers in summer.
**Tips and uses:** Flowers are used as a substitute for saffron spice. A red and yellow dye is made from the plant for use in cosmetics, food coloring, and textiles. The blooms work well as a cut flower, especially for winter bouquets. The color is striking in dried arrangements.
**Cultivar:** Not sold under variety name.

**Common name:** Sage, Mealy-cup; or Salvia
**Scientific name:** *Salvia farinacea*
**Plant hardiness:** Perennial grown as half-hardy annual. Zones 8–9.
**Optimal growing region and climate:** Very tolerant of high heat and humidity. Long-blooming plant. A native of New Mexico and Texas.
**Soil temperature for planting:** 70–85°F (21–29°C). Start seeds indoors 12 weeks before transplanting outdoors, after all danger of frost has passed.
**Soil needs:** Neutral, 7.0 pH, moist, well-drained soil. Fertility: average. Mix in decayed manure or humus.
**Light preference:** Full sun.
**Watering requirement:** Give plenty of water during dry spells.
**Spacing and size of plants:** 12–18 in. (30–45 cm) apart, to 2–3 ft. (60–90 cm) tall.
**Bloom period/season:** Blooms from early summer to frost.
**Tips and uses:** Good cutting flower and excellent for use in a mass planting. Works well as a background in gardens of mixed annuals. Deadhead to promote more blooms.
**Cultivars:** 'Alba,' 'Porcelaine,' 'Silver,' 'Strata,' Victoria'

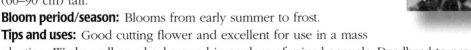

**Common name:** Silk Flower or Lady's Fingers
**Scientific name:** *Abelmoschus mochatus*
**Plant hardiness:** Perennial grown as tender annual. Zones 4–11.

**Optimal growing region and climate:** Flowers best in climates with long, hot summers. A relative of okra.

**Soil temperature for planting:** 75–80°F (24–27°C). Sow outdoors as soon as the ground warms and all danger of frost has passed; soak the seeds in warm water for an hour before planting. Late summer transplants will yield autumn flowers in mild-winter areas.

**Soil needs:** Neutral, 7.0 pH, moist, well-drained soil. Fertility: moderately rich.

**Light preference:** Full sun (or filtered shade in very hot areas).

**Watering requirement:** Water regularly, especially in hot-summer areas.

**Spacing and size of plants:** 12–18 in. (30–45 cm) apart, to 6 ft. (1.8 m) tall.

**Bloom period/season:** Summer to frost. Reliable bloom for up to 100 days after sowing.

**Tips and uses:** Can be grown as an indoor plant by a window with good light. Used in China as a headache medicine. A bushy plant for beds or borders.

**Cultivars:** 'Mischief,' 'Mischief Soft Pink'

**Common name:** Slipper Flower or Pocketbook Plant
**Scientific name:** *Calceolaria crenatiflora*
**Plant hardiness:** Half-hardy annual. Zones 3–10.
**Optimal growing region and climate:** Grows best in Pacific Northwest, coastal British Columbia, and at high altitudes. Best overall in mild-climate gardens; not heat resistant. Temperatures of 60–70°F (16–21°C) are ideal. Native to Chile and Peru.
**Soil temperature for planting:** 60°F (16°C). For spring color, start seeds indoors 12 weeks before the last frost. Also easy to grow from nursery transplants; set out as soon as all frost danger has passed.
**Soil needs:** Acid to neutral, 6.5–7.0 pH, well-drained soil. Fertility: moderately rich. Add compost or well-rotted manure.
**Light preference:** A partly shaded, cool location is best.
**Watering requirement:** Water regularly, keeping the soil moist but not wet.
**Spacing and size of plants:** 12 in. (30 cm) apart, to 18 in. (45 cm) tall.
**Bloom period/season:** Spring to summer.
**Tips and uses:** Good in containers or as a mass bed or border planting.
**Cultivars:** 'Anytime,' 'Sunshine'

**Common name:** Snapdragon
**Scientific name:** *Antirrhinum majus*
**Plant hardiness:** Half-hardy annual. Zones 2–10.
**Optimal growing region and climate:** Ideal outdoor temperature: 60–70°F (16–21°C); will tolerate some frost. Native to the Mediterranean.
**Soil temperature for planting:** 70–85°F (21–29°C). Sow seeds outdoors when soil is warm. Place transplants out in the early spring in cooler-weather climates. In mild areas, set transplants out in autumn.
**Soil needs:** Neutral, 7.0 pH, loose, loamy or sandy, well-drained soil. Fertility: rich. Feed monthly with diluted liquid plant food or fish emulsion fertilizer.

**Light preference:** Full sun.

**Watering requirement:** Keep soil moist.

**Spacing and size of plants:** 6–12 in. (15–30 cm) apart, to 2–3 ft. (60–90 cm) tall.

**Bloom period/season:** Winter to spring in mild-winter climates; spring to summer in cooler areas.

**Tips and uses:** Great for cutting and in beds. Available in dwarf, intermediate, and tall varieties. Pinch tips of plant to encourage bushy growth and abundant flowering.

**Cultivars:** 'Chinese Lanterns,' 'Madame Butterfly,' 'Sonnet,' 'Tahiti'

**Common name:** Snow-on-the-Mountain

**Scientific name:** *Euphorbia marginata*

**Plant hardiness:** Hardy annual. Zones 2–10.

**Optimal growing region and climate:** Native to the central U.S., from Texas to Minnesota. Prefers warmer weather. Tolerates heat and drought. Ideal outdoor temperature: 70–75°F (21–24°C).

**Soil temperature for planting:** 70°F (21°C). Avoid transplanting (plant contains a milky sap that can irritate skin, eyes, and open cuts). Best to sow seeds outdoors after the soil has warmed and all danger of frost has passed.

**Soil needs:** Neutral, 7.0 pH, well-drained soil. Fertility: poor to average. Does well within a wide range of soil conditions, from rich to poor and moist to dry. Tolerates limited care.

**Light preference:** Full sun to light shade.

**Watering requirement:** Water sparingly to moderately.

**Spacing and size of plants:** 8–12 in. (20–30 cm) apart, to 2 ft. (60 cm) tall; occasionally reaches 3–4 ft. (90–120 cm) tall.

**Bloom period/season:** Summer to autumn.

**Tips and uses:** As a cut flower, prepare stems immediately after cutting by searing the ends with a flame. An attractive border and bedding plant. Generally resistant of pests and disease.

**Cultivars:** 'Fireglow,' 'Polychroma,' 'Summer Icicle,' 'White Top'

**Common name:** Spider Flower

**Scientific name:** *Cleome hasslerana*

**Plant hardiness:** Half-hardy annual. Zones 2–11.

**Optimal growing region and climate:** Likes warm, humid conditions and lots of moisture but will withstand drought. Native to tropical America. Ideal outdoor temperature: 65–75°F (18–24°C).

**Soil temperature for planting:** 68–85°F (20–29°C). In areas with long, warm summers, sow seeds in early spring. In cooler zones, start seeds indoors 8–10 weeks before the last frost. Transplant when overnight soil temperatures exceed 50°F (10°C).

**Soil needs:** Neutral, 7.0 pH, moist, well-drained soil. Fertility: rich. Tolerates most soils.

**Light preference:** Full sun to light shade.

**Watering requirement:** Water frequently.

**Spacing and size of plants:** 18–24 in. (45–60 cm) apart, to 5 ft. (1.5 m) tall.

**Bloom period/season:** Summer to autumn frost.

**Tips and uses:** Resistant to pests and diseases. Works well for back of the border color or as a screen or hedge. Good cut flower. Attracts hummingbirds.

**Cultivars:** 'Cherry Queen,' 'Helen Campbell,' 'Pink Queen,' 'Queen Mixed Colors'

**Common name:** Statice, Sea Pink, or Sea Lavender
**Scientific name:** *Limonium sinuatum*
**Plant Hardiness:** Annual. Zones 4–11.
**Optimal growing region and climate:** An excellent choice for Pacific coastal gardens but also is tolerant of heat and drought. Native to the Mediterranean. Ideal outdoor temperature: 60–70°F (16–21°C).
**Soil temperature for planting:** 60–70°F (16–21°C). Start seeds indoors 8–10 weeks before last frost date. Sow seeds directly into the garden when all danger of frost has passed.
**Soil needs:** Neutral, 7.0 pH, well-drained, sandy loam. Fertility: average.
**Light preference:** Full sun.
**Watering requirement:** Water only when soil is dry to avoid root rot.
**Spacing and size of plants:** 9–12 in. (22–30 cm) apart, to 18 in. (45 cm) tall.
**Bloom period/season:** Summer to early autumn. Reliable blooms all summer in warm weather.
**Tips and uses:** To dry statice, cut stalks back just before the flowers are ready to open and tie the stems together in bunches. Hang bloom-end down in a cool, dry, and dark place. Cutting flowers encourages prolonged blooming.
**Cultivars:** 'Art Shades,' 'Grandstand,' 'Petite Bouquet'

**Common name:** Stock
**Scientific name:** *Matthiola incana*
**Plant hardiness:** Half-hardy annual, biennial, or perennial. Zones 2–9.
**Optimal growing region and climate:** A very cold-resistant plant that cannot bear heat. Needs a cool and moist environment to do well. Ceases blooming when temperature exceeds 73°F (23°C). Native to the Mediterranean coast.
**Soil temperature for planting:** 65–75°F (18–24°C). Start seeds 4–6 weeks before last frost. Sow seeds thickly since crowding encourages early bloom. Transplant outdoors when danger of heavy frost has passed. In mild climates, an outdoor sowing in late autumn provides a late-winter to spring bloom.
**Soil needs:** Neutral, 7.0 pH, moist, sandy, or loamy, well-drained soil. Fertility: moderately rich.
**Light preference:** Full sun to partial shade.
**Watering requirement:** Water with a fine spray when plants are becoming established, more profusely thereafter. Water in morning, when weather is cool. After plant matures, avoid watering foliage.
**Spacing and size of plants:** 12 in. (30 cm) apart, to 30 in. (75 cm) tall.
**Tips and uses:** Good in flower beds, borders, and for a cottage garden. Stock has a lovely spicy fragrance. Ideal for containers and cutting.
**Cultivars:** 'Cinderella,' 'Legacy,' 'Mammoth,' 'Midget'

**Common name:** Strawflower
**Scientific name:** *Helichrysum bracteatum*
**Plant hardiness:** Perennial grown as half-hardy annual. Zones 7-11.

**Optimal growing region and climate:** Does very well in areas with hot, dry summers. Avoid high-humidity regions where moisture can cause stem rot. Native to western Australia.

**Soil temperature for planting:** 60–70°F (16–21°C). For early blooms, start seeds indoors 6 weeks before the last frost date. Plant outside when frost danger has passed.

**Soil needs:** Neutral to alkaline, 7.0–7.5 pH, loamy or sandy, well-drained soil. Fertility: average to moderately rich. Tolerates poor soil as well as drought.

**Light preference:** Full sun.

**Watering requirement:** Water during dry spells; do not overwater.

**Spacing and size of plants:** 12 in. (30 cm) apart, to 3 ft. (90 cm) tall.

**Bloom period/season:** Summer to early autumn.

**Tips and uses:** A good cut flower for fresh arrangements and for dried arrangements because of its papery texture. Cut stalks before blooms open and hang flower-end down in a cool, dark place. Good in mixed beds, and borders.

**Cultivars:** 'Bright Bikinis Mix,' 'Dragon Hill Monarch,' 'Golden Star,' 'Harvest'

---

**Common name:** Sunflower, Common

**Scientific name:** *Helianthus annuus*

**Plant hardiness:** Hardy annual. Zones 4–9.

**Optimal growing region and climate:** Prefers warm weather and thrives under hot, dry conditions. Ideal outdoor temperature: 68–86°F (20–30°C). Native to North America.

**Soil temperature for planting:** 70–85°F (21–29°C). Grows very rapidly so there is no advantage to sowing indoors. Plant outdoors after all danger of frost has passed.

**Soil needs:** Neutral, 7.0 pH, moist, well-drained soil. Fertility: moderately rich. A fertile loam produces the largest flowers, but plant tolerates a wide range of soil conditions.

**Light preference:** Full sun.

**Watering requirement:** For lush growth, water well during hot spells.

**Spacing and size of plants:** 2 ft. (60 cm) apart, to 12 ft. (3.6 m) tall.

**Bloom period/season:** Summer.

**Tips and uses:** To save sunflower seeds for bird food, remove the flowerheads as soon as the seeds have matured. The birds will be happy to eat them off the plant as well. Works as a background plant in beds and borders.

**Cultivars:** 'Giganteus,' 'Italian White,' 'Sunburst,' 'Sunbright'

---

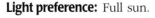

**Common name:** Sunflower, Mexican

**Scientific name:** *Tithonia rotundifolia*

**Plant hardiness:** Tender annual. Zones 9–11.

**Optimal growing region and climate:** Exceptionally resistant to very high heat and drought conditions. An excellent selection for a desert garden. Native to Mexico and Central America. Ideal outdoor temperature: 70–85°F (21–29°C).

**Soil temperature for planting:** 70°F (21°C). Start seeds indoors 6–8 weeks before the last frost. In mild-winter areas sow outdoors after all danger of frost has passed.

**Soil needs:** Neutral, 7.0 pH, well-drained soil. Fertility: average. Tolerates poor soils.

**Light preference:** Full sun.

**Watering requirement:** Water only during dry spells.
**Spacing and size of plants:** 2 ft. (60 cm) apart, grows to 6 ft. (1.8 m) tall.
**Bloom period/season:** Summer to early autumn. Fragrant, 3 in. (75 mm) blooms.
**Tips and uses:** Deadhead to prolong blooming. Attractive to butterflies and hummingbirds. Good for the back of the border, as a screen or hedge, along with common sunflowers. As a cut flower, close the hollow stems by searing them.
**Cultivars:** 'Aztec Sun,' 'Goldfinger,' 'Sundance,' 'Torch'

**Common name:** Sweet Pea
**Scientific name:** *Lathyrus odoratus*
**Plant hardiness:** Hardy annual. Zones 2–10.
**Optimal growing region and climate:** Does best in cool, moist climates but will perform well in warmer ones. Best areas are the northern Pacific and Atlantic coasts, including British Columbia and the maritime provinces of Canada. Ideal outdoor temperature: 55–65°F (13–18°C). Native to Italy.
**Soil temperature for planting:** 60–75°F (16–24°C). Plant in the spring as soon as danger of frost has passed and soil can be worked. In warmer zones, sow seeds from late summer to early autumn.
**Soil needs:** Neutral to alkaline, 7.0–7.5 pH, loamy, moist, well-drained soil. Fertility: rich. Enrich with humus but do not overfertilize.
**Light preference:** Full sun.
**Watering requirement:** Water regularly.
**Spacing and size of plants:** 6–12 in. (15–30 cm) apart, to 6 ft. (1.8 m) tall.
**Bloom period/season:** Spring to summer in cool-summer areas.
**Tips and uses:** The colorful varieties of this annual were hybridized in England during the Victorian age. Makes a good climbing vine and the blossoms are fragrant. Deadhead to encourage blooming. Grow in an area protected from wind.
**Cultivars:** 'Antique Factory,' 'Bijou Mixed,' 'Little Sweetheart,' 'Royal Family'`

**Common name:** Toad Flax
**Scientific name:** *Linaria maroccana*
**Plant hardiness:** Hardy annual. Zones 2–10.
**Optimal growing region and climate:** Prefers cool summers and a cooler clime overall. Native to Morocco.
**Soil temperature for planting:** 60°F (16°C). Sow outdoors as soon as the soil can be worked in the spring. Reseed every few weeks to keep fresh flowers blooming. An autumn sowing will yield winter to spring flowers in mild-winter zones.
**Soil needs:** Neutral, 7.0 pH, moist, well-drained, sandy soil. Fertility: rich. Tolerates most soils.
**Light preference:** Full sun to light shade.
**Watering requirement:** Water lightly; susceptible to root and stem rot.
**Spacing and size of plants:** 6 in. (15 cm) apart, to 18 in. (45 cm) tall.
**Bloom period/season:** Early spring through frost. Flowers winter through spring in mild-winter climates.
**Tips and uses:** Good rock garden or greenhouse plant. Nice cut flower. Deadhead after the first flowering. Generally resistant to pests and diseases.
**Cultivars:** 'Fairy Lights Mixed,' 'Fantasy,' 'Gemstones,' 'Northern Lights'

**Common name:** Tobacco, Flowering; or Nicotiana
**Scientific name:** *Nicotiana alata*
**Plant hardiness:** Half-hardy annual. Zones 2–10.
**Optimal growing region and climate:** Does very well in humid climates. Best where night temperatures are 50–60°F (10–16°C), daytime 70–75°F (21–24°C). Native to South America.

**Warning**

Foliage and sap of flowering tobacco poses hazard from poisoning. Avoid ingesting any part of the plant.

**Soil temperature for planting:** 70–85°F (21–29°C). Sow outdoors after last frost, or start seeds indoors 6–8 weeks before last frost date.
**Soil needs:** Neutral, 7.0 pH, moist, well-drained soil. Fertility: moderate. Fertilize every 2 weeks. Lime and potash are helpful additions.
**Light preference:** Full sun to partial shade.
**Watering requirement:** Water regularly; keep soil moist.
**Spacing and size of plants:** 12–24 in. (30–60 cm) apart, to 3–4½ ft. (0.9–1.4 m) tall.
**Bloom period/season:** Spring through frost.
**Tips and uses:** Best in borders, beds, and containers.
**Cultivars:** 'Grandiflora,' 'Jasmine Tobacco,' 'Starship Series,' 'Woodland Tobacco'

**Common name:** Gazania or Treasure Flower
**Scientific name:** *Gazania rigens*
**Plant Hardiness:** Perennial sometimes grown as an annual. Zones 3–11.
**Optimal growing region and climate:** Best in dry desert gardens where it will flower for months. Tolerates heat, drought, and wind. A South African native.
**Soil temperatures for planting:** 60°F (16°C). Start seeds indoors 6–8 weeks before final frost, then set them in a sunny spot.
**Soil needs:** Neutral, 7.0 pH, dry, sandy, very well-drained soil. Fertility: average. Tolerates poor soils.
**Light preference:** Full sun.
**Watering requirement:** Water only during dry spells. Avoid overwatering; it is susceptible to root rot and mildew.
**Spacing and size of plants:** 12 in. (30 cm) apart, to 16 in. (40 cm) tall.
**Bloom period/season:** Spring to summer bloom. Blooms close at night.
**Tips and uses:** Use in borders, beds, and containers. Also works well as edging and ground cover. Excellent in the drought-proof garden.
**Cultivars:** 'Golden Marguerita,' 'Mini Star Yellow,' 'Red Hybrids,' 'Sundance Hybrids'

**Common name:** Tree Mallow
**Scientific name:** *Lavatera trimestris*
**Plant hardiness:** Hardy annual. Zones 2–10.
**Optimal growing region and climate:** Ideal outdoor temperature: 70–75°F (21–24°C). Native to the Mediterranean.
**Soil temperature for planting:** 70°F (21°C). Avoid transplanting due to its extensive root system. Sow seeds outdoors in early spring, or after all danger of frost has passed.

**Soil needs:** Neutral, 7.0 pH, moist, well-drained, sandy soil. Fertility: average to moderately rich. Best flowers are produced in a dry, moderately rich soil. Add compost or well-rotted manure prior to planting.
**Light preference:** Full sun.
**Watering requirement:** Water only after soil becomes dry.
**Spacing and size of plants:** 2 ft. (60 cm) apart, to 3 ft. (90 cm) tall.
**Bloom period/season:** Summer to autumn frost.
**Tips and uses:** Good in mixed beds, borders, and in cutting gardens. Vulnerable to rust disease; dust with a sulfur-based fungicidal powder and remove infected leaves.
**Cultivars:** 'Loveliness,' 'Silver Cup,' 'Splendens,' 'Tanagra'

**Common name:** Trumpet Flower or Horn of Plenty
**Scientific name:** *Datura meteloides* and *D. inoxia*
**Plant hardiness:** Tender annual. Zones 3–11.
**Optimal growing region and climate:** A native of Central and tropical America. Does best in hot, sunny climates.
**Soil temperature for planting:** 65°F (18°C). Start seeds indoors 2–3 months before the last frost is due as plants are slow to develop. Transplant 2–3 weeks after all danger of frost has passed. In zones 9–11, it will grow all year long as long as there is only infrequent mild frost.

**Warning**

Avoid ingesting the seeds or sap of trumpet flower due to poison hazard.

**Soil needs:** Neutral, 7.0 pH, moist, well-drained soil. Fertility: best in an enriched soil. Feed weekly with a liquid fish emulsion fertilizer.
**Light preference:** Full sun.
**Watering requirement:** Keep soil moist.
**Spacing and size of plants:** 2 ft. (60 cm) apart, to 12 ft. (3.6 m) long.
**Bloom period/season:** Summer through autumn.
**Tips and uses:** Makes a nice container plant and a showy garden flower.
**Cultivars:** 'Alba,' 'Aurea,' 'Caerulea,' 'Cornucopaea,' 'Huberana'

**Common name:** Twinspur
**Scientific name:** *Diascia barberae*
**Plant hardiness:** Half-hardy annual. Zones 7–9.
**Optimal growing region and climate:** Prefers cool and dry conditions. Native to South Africa.
**Soil temperature for planting:** 60°F (16°C). Start seeds 6–8 weeks before the last frost, or sow seeds outdoors after all danger of frost has passed.
**Soil needs:** Neutral, 7.0 pH, moist, well-drained soil. Fertility: rich. Enrich with compost or well-rotted manure.
**Light preference:** Full sun.
**Watering requirement:** Water lightly to moderately whenever soil dries.
**Spacing and size of plants:** 6 in. (15 cm) apart, to 12 in. (30 cm) tall.
**Bloom period/season:** Summer to first frost.
**Tips and uses:** After first bloom of flowers has faded, cut all the flower stalks back to the foliage at the base of the plant for a second bloom. Nice in a border or rock garden.
**Cultivar:** 'Pink Queen'

**Common name:** Vinca
**Scientific name:** *Catharanthus roseus*
**Plant hardiness:** Tender annual. Zones 9–11.
**Optimal growing region and climate:** This native of Madagascar prefers warm weather—either hot and dry or hot and humid climates—and also is resistant to pollution. Frost tender. One of the best flowering annuals for desert regions.
**Soil temperature for planting:** 70–85°F (21–29°C). Set transplants out after the soil has warmed in the spring. Sow seeds indoors 12–16 weeks before soil as warmed. In very warm climates, seeds may be directly sown in the garden in late winter. Plant will self sow.
**Soil needs:** Neutral, 7.0 pH, moist, well-drained, sandy or loamy soil. Fertility: rich.
**Light preference:** Full sun to partial shade.
**Watering requirement:** Water regularly.
**Spacing and size of plants:** 9–12 in. (30 cm) apart, to 20 in. (50 cm) tall.
**Bloom period/season:** Late spring through autumn. In very warm zones, blooms year-round.
**Tips and uses:** Nice for beds, and as an attractive edging for a border. Works as a ground cover or in windowboxes. Doesn't need deadheading.
**Cultivars:** 'Little Linda,' 'Parasol,' 'Polka Dot,' 'Pretty in Pink'

**Common name:** Violet, Bush; Amethyst Browallia; or Lovely Browallia
**Scientific name:** *Browallia speciosa*
**Plant hardiness:** Perennial grown as tender annual. Zones 10–11.
**Optimal growing region and climate:** Does best in areas with very warm growing seasons. Originally found growing wild in the rainforests of Central America.
**Soil temperature for planting:** 70–85°F (21–29°C). Start indoors about 2 months before last frost.
**Soil needs:** Neutral, 7.0 pH, well-drained soil. Fertility: rich. Overfeeding leads to excessive foliage and fewer blooms.
**Light preference:** Partial to full shade. Full sun, if soil is cooled by frequent watering.
**Watering requirement:** Water by misting; do not overwater. If plant is in full sun, keep the soil very moist and cool.
**Spacing and size of plants:** 12 in. (30 cm) apart, to 5 ft. (1.5 m) tall.
**Bloom period/season:** Flowers late spring through summer.
**Tips and uses:** Pinch out young growth to encourage bushiness. Good plant for containers, hanging baskets, windowboxes, beds, and borders.
**Cultivars:** 'Blue Bells,' 'Heavenly Blue,' 'Jingle Bells,' 'Major,' 'Starlight'

**Common name:** Wishbone Flower
**Scientific name:** *Torenia fournieri*
**Plant hardiness:** Tender annual. Zones 4–11.
**Optimal growing region and climate:** A tropical and semi-tropical flower native of South Vietnam. Plant year-round in frost-free areas.
**Soil temperature for planting:** 70–85°F (21–29°C). Sow seeds after all danger of frost has passed and soil temperatures are 60°F (16°C) or higher. Start seeds indoors 6–8 weeks before final frost date.

**Soil needs:** Neutral, 7.0 pH, very moist but well-drained soil. Fertility: rich. Add peat moss or organic matter, especially if the soil has high clay or sand content.

**Light preference:** Full sun, in cooler climes; to full shade in warmest zones.

**Watering requirement:** Water regularly and well.

**Spacing and size of plants:** 6–8 in. (15–20 cm) apart, to 12 in. (30 cm) tall.

**Bloom period/season:** Summer to autumn.

**Tips and uses:** Good in borders, edges, rock gardens, hanging baskets, and containers. An excellent shade plant. Pinch back to promote bushy growth.

**Cultivars:** 'Clown Mix,' 'Panda'

**Common name:** Zinnia, Creeping
**Scientific name:** *Sanvitalia procumbens*
**Plant hardiness:** Tender annual. Zones 2–11.
**Optimal growing region and climate:** Native of Mexico that thrives in hot, humid weather. Drought tolerant.
**Soil temperature for planting:** 70–85°F (21–29°C). Sow in early spring upon the arrival of warm weather. Air temperatures must remain above 50°F (10°C) or the plant will not grow. In very mild areas, seeding can be done in autumn.
**Soil needs:** Neutral to alkaline, 7.0–7.5 pH, well-drained to dry, light soil. Fertility: average. Tolerates poor soils.
**Light preference:** Full sun.
**Watering requirement:** Once established, water minimally but do not allow soil to dry. Excessively dry plants will stop blooming.
**Spacing and size of plants:** 6–12 in. (15–30 cm) apart, to 8 in. (20 cm) tall.
**Bloom period/season:** Summer to autumn frost.
**Tips and uses:** Makes an excellent ground cover. Also attractive in rock gardens, borders, and windowboxes. Generally resistant to pests and diseases.
**Cultivars:** 'Gold Braid,' 'Mandarin Orange'

**Common name:** Zinnia, Garden
**Scientific name:** *Zinnia elegans*
**Plant hardiness:** Tender annual. Zones 4–11.
**Optimal growing region and climate:** America's most popular seed-grown flower relishes hot weather and is heat and drought tolerant. Native to Texas, Colorado, and Mexico.
**Soil temperature for planting:** 70–85°F (21–29°C). Avoid transplanting. Sow seeds when night temperatures remain above 50°F (10°C).
**Soil needs:** Neutral to alkaline, 7.0–7.5 pH, loamy, well-drained soil. Fertility: moderately rich. Fertilize lightly.
**Light preference:** Full sun.
**Watering requirement:** Water regularly, but avoid getting the foliage wet to prevent mildew from forming.
**Spacing and size of plants:** 6–12 in. (15–30 cm) apart, to 3 ft. (90 cm) tall.
**Bloom period/season:** Early summer to frost.
**Tips and uses:** The more flowers are cut back, the more they bloom. Works well as a cut flower. Excellent in borders, beds, and as an edger.
**Cultivars:** 'Blue Point Mix,' 'Short Stuff,' 'Thumbelina,' 'Yellow Ruffles'

**Understanding Annuals and Regional Climate Differences in Your Garden**

# Appendix

any plants that are treated as annuals in most of North America are not true annuals. To qualify as an annual, a plant must germinate, mature, set seed, and die in a year or less. A biennial completes the cycle from germination to termination in two years, growing foliage the first year and blooming the second; a number of popular annual-garden selections, such as sweet William, pinks, foxglove, hollyhock, and Canterbury bells, are actually biennials. Perennials survive for many seasons if the climate suits their needs. Several of North America's most-loved annual-garden selections—impatiens, geraniums, pansies, dahlias, and begonias among them—are perennials that survive from one year to the next in mild-winter climates.

These and all other plants are classified into two categories based on how they form seed leaves, or cotyledons. Most seed-bearing plants, including true annuals, are classified as dicots, which means that they form two seed leaves before their mature foliage emerges. Plants that form only one seed leaf are monocots. A few monocots, such as cannas and grasses, sometimes find their way into the annual garden. Plants also can be categorized according to how they reproduce. A plant propagated by means of underground buds is called a geophyte. Geophytes such as caladiums and tuberous begonias often are grown as annuals in areas where the freezing weather kills their roots and underground buds.

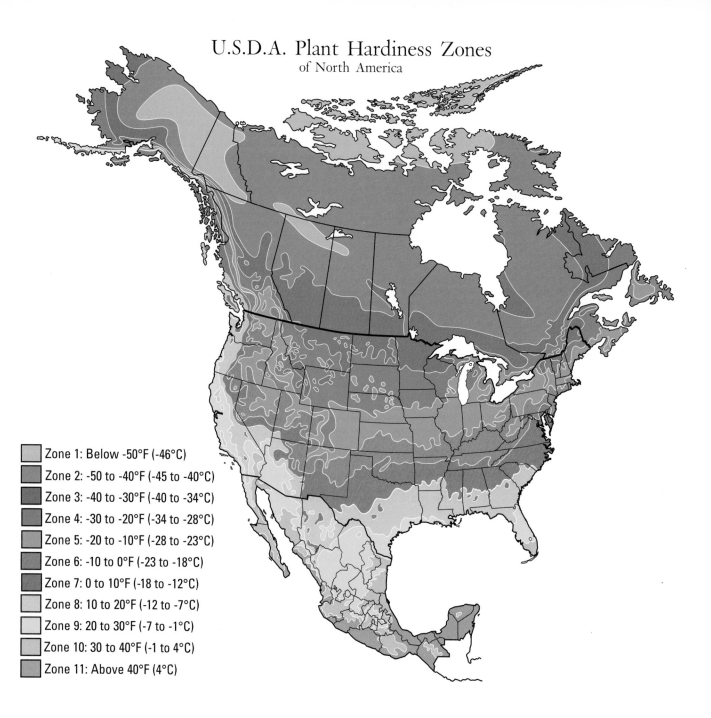

# U.S.D.A. Plant Hardiness Zones
## of North America

- Zone 1: Below -50°F (-46°C)
- Zone 2: -50 to -40°F (-45 to -40°C)
- Zone 3: -40 to -30°F (-40 to -34°C)
- Zone 4: -30 to -20°F (-34 to -28°C)
- Zone 5: -20 to -10°F (-28 to -23°C)
- Zone 6: -10 to 0°F (-23 to -18°C)
- Zone 7: 0 to 10°F (-18 to -12°C)
- Zone 8: 10 to 20°F (-12 to -7°C)
- Zone 9: 20 to 30°F (-7 to -1°C)
- Zone 10: 30 to 40°F (-1 to 4°C)
- Zone 11: Above 40°F (4°C)

## Plant Hardiness Zones

The United States Department of Agriculture (USDA) Plant Hardiness Zone Map provides a general guide to growing conditions in North America. It divides the continent into 11 zones based on average minimum annual temperatures within each zone. The zones roughly predict which plants will adapt to a given area.

While a true annual is genetically programmed to survive for no more than a year regardless of where it's planted, a perennial or biennial will live on in zones where they've adapted to the climate. In other zones, perennials and biennials will behave as true annuals, dying at the end of the season. Many species that are perennial in zones 9, 10, and 11 are planted as summer annuals in zones where they can't live through the winter.

When you're planting a garden that's intended to last for a single season—whether you're planning for true annuals, or for using perennials and biennials as annuals—you don't need to worry about minimum temperatures. Your major concern is the first and last frost dates in your area [see chart, opposite]. As long as you know when the last spring frost occurs in your area, you can sow hardy annuals six weeks before the last frost and tender ones a couple of weeks later when soils warm. Tender annuals, and tender perennials used as annuals in cold-winter climates, will die with the first autumn frost. The average first and last frost dates for your area are guidelines, however, not guarantees.

Moreover, zone maps and frost charts alike can't account for the effects of thermal belts, nearby bodies of water, and other factors that create microclimates within zones. Only careful observation will give you an accurate picture of climatic conditions in your own backyard.

### Climate

Severe cold or heat can doom many plants, and even a short bout of pelting rain or punishing wind can wreak havoc in a garden. To see your plants through such tough times, give them a fighting chance against the normal vicissitudes of weather when they're little and stand ready to protect them from extreme conditions as they grow.

The best way to prevent weather-induced garden failure is to put your plants in the ground at the proper time. Hardy annuals (and biennials grown as hardy annuals) can be sown indoors six weeks before the last frost in your area; tender annuals (including tender perennials grown as annuals) shouldn't be planted until two weeks after the average last-frost date, and checking soil temperatures. Warm-season species planted too early may be killed by cold or may never germinate; cool-season ones planted too late will have limited blooms or fail in summer heat.

---

**Approximate Frost-free Dates**

Zone 1 . . . . . . . . .July 20–August 31
Zone 2 . . . . . . .July 10–September 10
Zone 3 . . . . .June 30–September 15
Zone 4 . . . . .June 15–September 25
Zone 5 . . . . . . .May 25–October 10
Zone 6 . . . . . . .May 15–October 20
Zone 7 . . . . . .April 25–November 1
Zone 8 . . . . .April 15–November 10
Zone 9 . . . .March 15–November 15
Zone 10 . .February 10–December 10
Zone 11 . . . . . . .Frost-free All Year

---

Hardening, the process of acclimating seedlings, is an important preventive measure that helps young plants make the transition from a controlled indoor environment to the garden, where they will have to withstand temperature changes, direct sunlight, and drying wind. Plants that are hardened properly are better equipped to survive severe weather; otherwise, they may be damaged or even killed by normal weather conditions.

When the wind comes up, tall plants will be spared significant damage if they've been staked from the time they were young. However, not much can save plants from gale-force winds. If your area is prone to these, sow tall and slender-stemmed, large-flowered plants only in sheltered areas.

Despite a gardener's best-laid plans and prophylactic measures, nature is bound to have some challenging surprises in store. If harsh weather threatens before your plants are in the ground, the solution is simple: when the temperature falls below 50°F (10°C), a heat wave is on the way, or a wind- or rainstorm is due, bring your plants indoors or protect them in a cold frame.

If your garden is already planted, you'll need to protect it until the danger passes. A floating row cover—a lightweight polyester blanket that can be put right over your plants—will hold in daytime heat and provide insulation during an unexpected cold snap. A floating row cover also can be useful when you have the opposite problem—too much heat—since it holds in moisture and filters out 20–25 percent of sunlight. When the weather gets very hot, you'll need to come to the rescue with extra waterings; this is also the remedy for windy days, and will help protect the plants from drying out. During a severe heat spell, you may need to water your garden several times a day. However, if you live in a place where the summer is one long heat spell, it isn't practical to take such heroic measures every day. Look for species known for their heat and drought tolerance to keep watering chores within reason.

### Sun Exposure

Plants that have been grown with artificial light need to be exposed to sunlight gradually or they will burn. To protect young plants—whether you've purchased them as seedlings or grown them indoors yourself—be sure to harden the plants before you put them in the garden.

Hardening is the process of slowly acclimating delicate seedlings to the outdoors. The transition from a protected indoor environment to the rough-and-tumble of garden living takes several days. Leave plants outside for a little longer each day until they're spending all of their time outdoors.

When you harden plants, you're getting them accustomed to sunlight, not just temperature changes. When you first bring them outdoors, or when you get them home, put them in a shady, protected place. Expose them to a little more sunlight each time you move them outdoors, rotating them through increasingly sunny locations until they're spending all day in the sun (shade-loving plants shouldn't be put in direct sun at all—just move them from their protected outdoor area to their planting site for a little longer every day). If you're using a cold frame to harden off your plants, put a piece of screen across its translucent cover to create some shade. Leave the cover closed when you first bring plants outdoors, then open it for a bit longer each day.

### Growth Habits

Choosing a plant is a little like shopping for a puppy: you need to keep in mind that it will look different when it's full-grown. By thinking ahead, you'll be creating a garden instead of collecting a random assortment of specimens that enticed you at the nursery. If you like a plant, take the time to find out whether it will attain the proportions of a great dane or a chihuahua. At the same time, make sure that it will adapt to the conditions in your yard and bloom when you want.

All annuals start out as seeds, but some grow to be bushy or spiky, others trail along the ground, and still others form neat, low mounds. These traits, which gardeners call "habits," are depicted in Annual Plants and Tender Perennials [see pg. 91]. You'll often find such information on seed packages or plant tags as well. Consult these sources before you buy so you can keep your plants in scale with their ultimate surroundings and assemble a pleasing mix of forms. Also consult with the experts at your local nursery or garden retail store.

In addition, your research will tell you about the growing conditions your plants need. Check to see whether they prefer sun or shade, and what kind of soil they require. Armed with this information, you can visit the local nursery looking for plants that interest you and meet the needs of your intended planting site.

Since plants that flower in late summer won't do if you long for spring blossoms, you'll want to find out exactly what annuals to plant in which season. The encyclopedia lists the planting and bloom times for annuals in each North American growing zone; seed packages and plant tags may offer more general information, for example, that a plant "blooms from late spring to fall frost." Keep in mind that with annuals you can have it all—plant a spring garden of cool-season annuals, a summer garden of warm-season species, or a mixture of both for a seasonal progression of blooms.

### Soil

Because plants absorb air, moisture, and nutrients through their roots, the single most important element of a successful garden is excellent soil. If the soil is too dense, plants can't absorb what they need and their roots will rot; if the soil is too loose and grainy, water will drain right through, taking nutrients with it.

There are three basic types of soil: clay, sand, and loam. To determine which of these you have in your garden, pick up a handful of moistened soil and squeeze it. If it feels heavy and sticky and retains its shape, you have a soil that is mostly clay. If it feels gritty and falls through your fingers, you have sandy soil. If it forms a ball that crumbles when you touch it, you've got loam, the ideal soil for growing annuals (and most other plants). Confirm your diagnosis by doing a drainage test: dig a hole about the size of a 1-gallon (3.8-l) flower pot and fill it with water. Loamy soil will drain at the rate of about an inch (25 mm) per hour; clay will drain significantly more slowly, and sandy soils much more quickly.

Creating loam for your plants may require adding compost or other organic material. If you're starting a garden from scratch, clear away all vegetation before you begin digging. Be sure to remove any roots so that weeds and grasses don't rise up to plague you. This will be easier to do if the ground is moist, so three to four days before you plan to work the soil, soak it thoroughly. When its texture is crumbly but not sticky, use a spade, fork, or rototiller to turn over 8–12 inches (20–30 cm) of soil, removing rocks and breaking up clumps as you go. Cover the whole bed with a 2-inch (5-cm) layer of compost, which will improve drainage in clay soil and help sandy soil retain moisture. Add lime or sulfur if your soil's pH needs correcting, along with a pound (0.5 kg) of fertilizer for every hundred square feet (9 m$^2$) of planting space. Finally, dig the bed a second time, working all amendments into the soil.

Since annuals have shallow roots, this will be sufficient preparation. If you're starting a mixed bed of annuals and perennials, you'll need to lift and loosen the soil to a depth equal to two spades—a minimum of 15 inches (38 cm)—in a process known as double digging. To double dig your bed, spade or till an 8-inch (20-cm) layer of soil and shovel it aside, then turn over another 8-inch (20 cm) layer and work in plenty of organic material and lime or sulfur, as you did for single digging. Replace the top layer, dig in more amendments, and water the bed thoroughly. This process also will be necessary if you hit hardpan, a layer of very dense subsoil, within 10 inches (25 cm) of the soil's surface. In that case, completely remove the hard subsoil to a depth of 15 inches (38 cm), fill the resulting hole with imported topsoil and compost, then replace the subsoil atop the bed and work in more amendments.

Another option is to create a raised bed, which can involve building a frame and filling it with soil and organic material, or may be just a simple matter of depositing a heap of topsoil and compost on top of the native soil. If your planting site has very poor drainage, a raised bed may be your only option, since it's nearly impossible to turn a swampy corner of the yard into a garden through addition of soil amendments alone.

Should you have garden failures, check first whether soil is the cause. If plants turn yellow or bloom poorly, they may be getting too little nitrogen from the soil, or an improper pH level may be preventing them from absorbing micronutrients. If they suddenly wilt and die, soggy soil may be harboring the fungus that causes root rot. Preserve the quality of your soil and prevent future problems by using organic mulches, preserving topsoil when you weed, and rotating crops so the soil doesn't become a breeding ground for disease.

## Watering

As a rule, plants need about an inch (25 mm) of water per week to grow and bloom. They do best when their roots are deeply watered and allowed to dry out a bit between waterings; frequent light sprinklings will cause them to form too-shallow root systems, which will weaken them and increase their susceptibility to pests and disease.

In general, watering is best accomplished with a soaker hose or irrigation system rather than an overhead spray from a garden hose. A sprinkler can provide enough moisture, but the overhead watering will make leaves vulnerable to powdery mildew when weather is cool. To determine whether your system is providing adequate water, use a rain gauge or dig down with a trowel to see whether the soil is moist to a depth of 6 inches (20 cm). Never water to the point of sogginess, which creates a hospitable environment for the fungi that cause damping off and root rot. On the other hand, don't allow plants to become too dry or you'll be putting out the welcome mat for insects. A good rule of thumb is to water whenever the top 2–3 inches (5–8 cm) of soil become dry.

If you live in a climate where water is scarce, or you simply dislike the chore of watering, you can fill your garden with plants that tolerate underwatering, including African daisy, vinca, cape marigold, Dahlberg daisy, California poppy, snow-on-the-mountain, and coreopsis. If you live in an area with frequent rainfall, you have fewer choices. Only a few annual-garden flowers truly thrive in moist soil, notably monkey flower and forget-me-not. Other selections that will tolerate somewhat moist conditions are vinca, spider flower, castor bean, wishbone flower, nasturtium, and pansy. To achieve best results, amend too-damp soil with abundant organic compost, adding gypsum if the soil is mostly clay.

# ON-LINE INDEX

(www.botany.com) Botany.Com. Excellent plant encyclopedia.

(www.gardenweb.com) GardenWeb. Extensive forums, links, seed exchange.

(www.garden-gate.prairienet.org) Garden Gate. Special Midwest-oriented resources.

(www.almanac.com/garden) The Old Farmer's Almanac.

(www.sierra.com/sierrahome/gardening) SierraHome.Com. Gardening software.

(www.plants.usda.gov) United States Department of Agriculture.

(www.homearts.com) HomeArts: Plant encyclopedia, discussion forums.

(www.rebeccasgarden.com) Rebecca's Garden. Link to the television show.

(www.gardenguides.com) Garden Guides. Flower, vegetable, and herb.

(www.backyardgardener.com) Backyard Gardener. Alpine, perennials, annuals.

(www.vg.com) Virtual Garden: Where Gardens Grow. Zone locator.

(www.gardennet.com) GardenNet. Plant information by type and group.

(www.gardentown.com) GardenTown. Message board and chat, Canadian input.

(www.nws.noaa.gov) National Weather Service home page. Current conditions.

(www.plantamerica.com) PlantAmerica: Multimedia tools for garden design.

(www.tpoint.net/neighbor) or (www.io.com/neighbor) The Gardening Launch Pad.

(www.mastercomposter.com) Master Composter. Composting advice.

(www.garden.com) Garden.Com. Shopping, magazines, tips, chat, seeds, tools, accessories, books, zones.

## A

*Abelmoschus mochatus*, 119–120
*Ageratum houstonianum*, 104
*Alcea rosea*, 106–107
African Daisy, 44, 101
Alyssum, Sweet, 3, 10, 22, 23, 64, 92
Amaranth, Globe, 3, 9, 31, 92
*Amaranthus caudatus*, 109–110
Amethyst Browallia, 127
Annual Chrysanthemum, 98–99
Annual Delphinium, 108
*Antirrhinum majus*, 120–121
*Arctotis stoechadifolia*, 101
Aster, China, 10, 80, 92–93
*Atriplex hortensis*, 44

## B

Baby Blue Eyes, 93
Baby's Breath, 93
Bachelor's Button, 64, 94
Balm, Molucca, 94–95
Basil, 6, 90
Begonia, 5, 6, 12, 13, 16, 23, 44, 129
Begonia, Wax, 94
*Begonia* ✕ *semperflorens-cultorum*, 94
Bellflower, Serbian, 21
Bells, Canterbury, 129
Bells of Ireland, 7, 94–95
Birds, 17
Black-eyed Susan, 11, 13, 17, 48, 51, 95
Black-eyed Susan Vine, 95
Blanket Flower, 95–96
Bloodleaf, 44
Bluebonnet, Texas, 96
Bluebird, 114
Bluebottle, 94
Borders, 8, 9, 46, 47
 English, 2–5, 50
 seeds, 25
Bouquets, 85, 86–87
*Browallia speciosa*, 127
*Brachycome iberidifolia*, 102
*Brassica oleracea*, 108
Browallia, Amethyst, 127
Browallia, Lovely, 15, 127
Bush Violet, 127
Busy Lizzie, 107
Butterflies, 17
Butterfly Flower, 12, 96–97

## C

Cabbage, Ornamental, 6, 108
Caladium, 12, 129
*Calceolaria crenatiflora*, 120
Calendula, 6, 64, 76, 90
*Calendula officinalis*, 111

California Poppy, 117
Calliopsis, 97
*Callistephus chinensis*, 92–93
Campion, 118–119
Candytuft, Globe, 64, 97
Canna, 6, 44
Canterbury Bells, 129
*Capsicum annuum*, 115
Carnation, Pink, 97–98
*Carthamus tinctorius*, 119
Castor Bean, 15, 24, 44, 98
Castor Oil Plant, 98
Catalogs, 34–35
*Catharanthus roseus*, 127
Celosia, 15, 31
Celosia, Plumed, 64, 99–100
*Celosia cristata*, 99–100
*Centaurea cyanus*, 94
Cherry Pie, 106
Children, 1, 85, 89
China Aster, 10, 80, 92–93
China Pink, 97–98
Christmas Pepper, 115
Chrysanthemum, Annual, 14, 98–99
*Chrysanthemum multicaule*, 98–99
Cineraria, 102
Clarkia, 99
*Clarkia amoena*, 99
Clematis, 23
*Cleome hasslerana*, 121
Cockscomb, Crested, 6, 8, 99–100
Coleus, Garden, 15, 44, 100
*Coleus* ✕ *hybridus*, 100
Color wheel, 40–42
*Consolida ambigua*, 108
Containers, 7, 13, 19
 moving, 26
 planting in, 62–63
 seeds, 60–62
 transplants, 71
 windowboxes, 52
*Convolvulus tricolor*, 112–113
Coreopsis, 3, 9, 11, 17, 48, 97
*Coreopsis tinctoria*, 97
Cornflower, 11, 48, 94
Cosmos, 4, 15, 64, 100
 *Cosmos bipinnatus*, 100
 *Cosmos sulphureus*, 100
Creeping Zinnia, 128
Crested Cockscomb, 99
*Cuphea ignea*, 103

## D

Daffodils, 21
Dahlberg Daisy, 101–102
Dahlia, Annual, 7, 15, 16, 44, 86, 100–101, 129

# INDEX

*Dahlia* ✕ *hybrida*, 100–101
Daisies
    Daisies, gloriosa, 6
    Daisy, African, 44, 101
    Daisy, Dahlberg, 48, 101–102
    Daisy, English, 6
    Daisy, Swan River, 48, 102
*Datura inoxia*, 126
*Datura meteloides*, 126
Delphinium, Annual, 108
*Dianthus chinensis*, 97–98
*Diascia barberae*, 126
*Dimorphotheca pluvialis*, 111
Disease, 29, 55, 60, 73, 81–83
Drainage, 19, 30
Dusty Miller, 44, 90, 102
Dwarf Morning Glory, 112
*Dyssodia tenuiloba*, 101–102

## E

Elephant's Ear, 27
English borders, 2–5, 8, 9, 27, 50
English daisies, 14
*Eschscholzia californica*, 117
*Euphorbia marginata*, 121
Everlasting, 102–103

## F

False Saffron, 119
Felicias, 15
Fertilizing, 55, 73, 77–79
Firecracker Plant, 103
Flame Nettle, 100
Flanders Poppy, 117
Flax, Flowering, 2, 103–104
Flowering Flax, 2, 103–104
Flowering Tobacco, 125
Fleece, Golden, 101–102
Flossflower, 7, 15, 104
Forget-Me-Not, Garden, 11, 12, 14, 17,
    23, 104
Four O'clock, 16, 17, 105
Foxglove, 2, 21, 129
Frost, 20–21. *See also* Temperature

## G

*Gaillardia pulchella*, 95–96
Garden Coleus, 100
Garden Forget-Me-Not, 104
Garden Nasturtium, 113
Gazania, 78, 125
*Gazania regens*, 125
Geranium, Common, 10, 15, 16, 42, 105,
    129
Geranium, Trailing, 105–106
Gifts, 7, 90

Globe Amaranth, 3, 9, 31, 92
Globe Candytuft, 64
Godetia, 99
Golden Fleece, 101–102
*Gomphrena globosa*, 92
*Gypsophila elegans*, 93

## H

Hardening, 66, 67. *See also* Temperature
Hedges, 4. *See also* Borders
*Helianthus annuus*, 123
*Helichrysum bracteatum*, 122–123
Heliotrope, 16, 106
*Heliotropium arborescens*, 106
*Helipterum roseum*, 102–103
*Hibiscus acetosella*, 44
Hollyhock, 90, 106–107, 129
Horn of Plenty, 126
Humidity, 9, 23. *See also* Temperature
Hyacinth, 6

## I

*Iberis umbellata*, 97
Iceland Poppy, 117
Impatiens, 5, 12, 13, 15, 107, 129
*Impatiens wallerana*, 107
Insects, 6, 55, 73, 81–83
*Ipomoea batatas*, 44
Irrigation, 68–69. *See also* Watering
*Irsine herbstii*, 44
Ivy Geranium, 7

## J

Johnny-Jump-Up, 10, 12, 14, 107

## K

Kale, Ornamental, 44, 108

## L

Lady's Fingers, 119–120
Larkspur, Rocket, 5, 12, 14, 31, 42, 108
*Lathyrus odoratus*, 124
*Lavatera trimestris*, 125–126
Lavender, Sea, 122
*Limonium sinuatum*, 122
*Linaria maroccana*, 124
*Linum grandiflorum*, 103–104
Lisianthus, 10, 22
Lobelia, 7, 12, 15, 16, 44, 108–109
*Lobelia erinus*, 108–109
*Lobularia maritima*, 92
Love-in-a-Mist, 5, 27, 44, 109
Love-Lies-Bleeding, 8, 78, 109–110
Lovely Browallia, 127
Lupine, 96

*Lupinus texensis*, 96
*Lychnis coeli-rosa*, 118–119

## M

Mallow Wort, 110
*Malope trifida*, 110
Marigold, 6, 15, 17, 45, 64, 90, 110
    Marigold, Cape, 111
    Marigold, Pot, 111
Marvel of Peru, 105
*Matthiola incana*, 122
Meadow Foam, 12, 23
Mealy-cup Sage, 119
Mexican Sunflower, 3, 8, 15, 86, 123–124
Mignonette, Common, 111–112
*Mimulus hybridus*, 112
*Mirabilis jalapa*, 105
Molucca Balm, 94–95
*Molucella laevis*, 94–95
Monkey Flower, 23, 112
Morning Glory, 15, 16, 24, 27
Morning Glory, Dwarf, 112–113
Moss Rose, 7, 9, 13, 17, 23, 31, 64, 78,
    113
Mulch, 70
Mustard, Red, 6
*Myosotis sylvatica*, 104

## N

Nasturtium, Garden, 6, 64, 78, 113
Nemesia, Pouch, 114
*Nemesia strumosa*, 114
*Nemophila menziesii*, 93
Nettle, Flame, 100
New Guinea, 12
Nicotiana, 12, 16, 45, 64, 125
*Nicotiana alata*, 125
*Nigella damascena*, 109

## O

Organic, 33
Ornamental Cabbage, 6, 108
Ornamental Kale, 108
Ornamental Pepper, 115

## P

Painted Tongue, 114
Pansy, 2, 3, 6, 10, 14, 48, 114–115, 129
*Papaver nudicaule*, 117–118
*Papaver rhoeas*, 117
Pathways, 53
*Pelargonium peltatum*, 105–106
*Pelargonium* ✕ *hortorum*, 105
Pepper, Christmas, 115
Pepper, Ornamental, 115
*Perilla frutescens*, 44

# INDEX

Periwinkle, 13, 16, 27, 31, 44
Pesticides, 33
Pests, 6, 55, 73, 81–83
Petunia, 7, 10, 15, 16, 22, 76, 90, 115–116
*Petunia* X *hybrida*, 115–116
pH, 30
Phlox, 64, 116
*Phlox drummondii*, 116
Pie, Cherry, 106
Pincushion Flower, 116
Pink, China, 97–98
Pink, Sea, 122
Planning, 25, 39, 49, 51, 53
    color, 40–42, 85, 88
    containers, 26 (*See also* Containers)
Plectranthus, 12
Plumed Celosia, 99–100
Pocketbook Plant, 120
Polka Dot Plant, 12
Pollution, 9
Poor Man's Orchid, 96–97
Poppy, 14, 24, 86
    Poppy, California, 11, 117
    Poppy, Flanders, 117
    Poppy, Iceland, 2, 117–118
    Poppy, Shirley, 117
*Portulaca grandiflora*, 113
Pot Marigold, 111
Pots. See Containers
Potting table, 55, 56, 57–59
Pouch Nemesia, 114
Presents, 7, 90
Primrose, 6, 118
*Primula malacoides*, 118
Pruning, 55, 73, 80

## R

Raised beds, 30
Red Orach, 44
*Reseda odorata*, 111–112
*Ricinus communis*, 98
Rocket Larkspur, 108
Rose-of-Heaven, 118–119
*Rudbeckia hirta*, 95

## S

Safflower, 119
Saffron, False, 119
Sage, Mealy-cup, 119
*Salpiglossis sinuata*, 114
Salvia, 15, 16, 51, 64, 119
    *Salvia farinacea*, 119
    *Salvia officinalis*, 44
*Sanvitalia procumbens*, 128
*Scabiosa atropurpurea*, 116
Scabious, Sweet, 116
*Schizanthus pinnatus*, 96–97

Sea Lavender, 122
Sea Pink, 122
Seedlings, 28–29
Seeds, 28, 55
    beds, 64–65
    containers, 60–62 (*See also* Containers)
*Senecio* X *hybridus*, 102
Serbian Bellflower, 21
Shade, 27
Shellflower, 94–95
Shirley Poppy, 117
Signet Marigold, 4
Silk Flower, 119–120
Slipper Flower, 120
Snapdragon, 3, 8, 16, 75, 120–121
Snow-on-the-Mountain, 121
Soil, 9, 12, 25, 30–31
Spacing, 29
Spider Flower, 3, 6, 12, 15, 78, 121
Statice, 122
Stock, 122
Strawflower, 102–103, 122-123
Sunflower, Common, 4, 6, 17, 27, 44, 64, 123
Sunflower, Mexican, 3, 8, 15, 86, 123–124
Supports, 73, 74
Sweet Alyssum, 3, 10, 22, 23, 64, 92
Sweet Pea, 124
Sweet Scabious, 116
Sweet William, 2, 129

## T

Table, potting, 55, 56, 57–59
*Tagetes erecta*, 110
Tassel Flower, 109–110
Temperature, 8, 9–10, 20, 21, 43
    borders, 2–3, 5 (*See also* Borders)
    frost, 20–21, 43
    hardening, 66, 67
    transplants, 66
Testing, soil 30
Texas Bluebonnet, 96
*Thunbergia alata*, 95
*Tithonia rotundifolia*, 123–124
Toad Flax, 124
Tobacco, Flowering, 125
Tools, 32–33, 34, 56
*Torenia fournieri*, 127–128
Trailing Geranium, 105
Transplants, 20, 63
    containers, 71
    hardening, 66, 67
Treasure Flower, 125
Tree Mallow, 125–126
Trellis, 23
*Tropaeolum majus*, 113
Trumpet Flower, 126

Tuberous, 129
Twinspur, 126

## V

Vegetables, 6
Velvet Flower, 114
Verbena, 5
Vinca, 127
Viola, 13, 48
    *Viola cornuta*, 114–115
    *Viola tricolor*, 107
Violet, Bush, 13, 127
Viscaria, 12, 13

## W

Walkways, 53
Wallflower, 12
Watering, 9, 25, 29, 55, 73, 75–76
    drip, 68–69
    irrigation, 68–69
Wax Begonia, 94
Wishbone Flower, 127–128

## Z

Zinnia, 6, 15, 16, 23, 27, 43, 64, 76
    Zinnia, Creeping, 7, 9, 128
    Zinnia, Garden, 128
    *Zinnia elegans*, 128